Organizational Change in Practice

This book challenges the practice of organizational change programmes. It uses two case studies in depth to illustrate that consulting companies can often get it wrong. Senior managers often do not know enough about managing change. The text is arranged around eight deadly sins to avoid in the practice of change: self-deception of the change agents rather than self-awareness; destruction of the identity of the organization caused by arrogance, especially of the large consulting companies; destruction of cohesion; gobbledygook language; concentrating on structural change, not behavioural change; making the organization worse, not better; the intelligence in resistance; and the deep trauma of redundancy.

The author's main objective is to get academics and practitioners to stop and think about what they are doing when they work with organizations. *Organizational Change in Practice* will be of interest to business professionals seeking to understand how change can impact their organization as well as organizational consultants.

Dr Annamaria Garden is an independent organizational consultant. She has over 20 years' experience in the field of organizational change and has experience running her own self-employed consulting and facilitation practice in London, gaining a reputation for being creative, leading edge and dependable.

Organizational Change in Practice

The Eight Deadly Sins Preventing Effective Change

Annamaria Garden

LONDON AND NEW YORK

First published 2017
by Routledge
2 Park Square, Milton Park, Abingdon, Oxon OX14 4RN

and by Routledge
711 Third Avenue, New York, NY 10017

Routledge is an imprint of the Taylor & Francis Group, an informa business

British Library Cataloguing-in-Publication Data
A catalogue record for this book is available from the British Library

Library of Congress Cataloguing-in-Publication Data
Names: Garden, Anna-Maria, author.
Title: Organizational change in practice : the eight deadly sins preventing effective change / Annamaria Garden.
Description: 1 Edition. | New York : Routledge, 2017. | Includes bibliographical references and index.
Identifiers: LCCN 2016053002 | ISBN 9780415790154 (hardback) | ISBN 9781315213569 (ebook)
Subjects: LCSH: Organizational change. | Strategic planning.
Classification: LCC HD58.8 .G3677 2017 | DDC 658.4/06—dc23
LC record available at https://lccn.loc.gov/2016053002

ISBN: 978-0-415-79015-4 (hbk)
ISBN: 978-1-315-21356-9 (ebk)

Typeset in Times New Roman
by Apex CoVantage, LLC

Contents

Figures

Tables

Checklists

Acknowledgements

The Illustration for Figure 6.2 has been kindly and expertly done by Neil White. Excerpts from the case study in Chapter 1 of *Reading the Mind of the Organization* by this author and published by Gower Publishing Limited, Hampshire, UK, 2000 are published in segments through the present book. Permission has been granted.

Introduction

It has become trite to acknowledge that, at one and the same time, organizations are engaging in an unprecedented level of change programmes, but that the majority of change efforts are failing (Kotter and Cohen, 1995; Beer and Nohria, 2011; Hamel and Zanini, 2014). News of this dichotomy doesn't seem to faze organizations who carry on regardless. At the heart of these change efforts is the belief and assumption that 'change' is 'better'. This is why people using the word 'change' expect you to 'get it' and support the change effort. However, organizational change is not always and everywhere good. In this book, I try to distinguish between those instances when change is indeed better and when it is decidedly worse. My intention is to boost those change efforts which are good and productive and to reduce those change efforts that are not.

I am one of those consultants who has, for two decades, spent most of my work time on change processes, usually focusing on behaviour change to suit the strategy change. I don't see my efforts as having been wasted. That may be precisely because I was engaged with behaviour change and it is failure to do so which seems to be a key determinant of a change effort failure. That may have been also because I focused on the soft stuff while others – partners in a network of consultants – were oriented at the same time to the hard stuff (see Beer and Nohria, 2011).

In addition, however, to my typical consulting adventures, I have had two close encounters with two large consulting companies in client or employing organizations. In what follows in this book, I use these two examples as examples of what *not* to do in a change effort.

Years before, two journalists wrote a book, titled *The Witchdoctors* (Micklethwait and Wooldridge, 1996). Their book is pitched at unearthing the good in management consulting and management gurus amidst the rubble of all that is wrong. They pay particular attention to 'management speak' and fads. My own book, insofar as my two main case studies are concerned, follows in the train of *The Witchdoctors* as I look aghast at the two cases and try to extract what is useful in the practice of change. A few years later, I am still haunted by the consultant's incompetence as well as the cruelty (lack of emotional quotient). Was the behaviour of these two consulting companies a one-off or was it standard? No matter, they serve as useful learning vehicles of this book. They taught me the eight deadly sins preventing effective change.

For example, one company was a client in London where they were launching into a programme called 'transformation' (a word used frequently but not meaningfully). This was aimed at transforming the whole company from strategy to processes to culture. Instead, first, the change team destroyed the cohesion in the company; second, no strategy was determined because of the upheaval in the company; third, a Holy War erupted between the change team and one of the key divisions; finally, they tried to alter the identity of the company but they weren't really aware that they were doing that.

In the second example, I was caught up in a 're-alignment' (a word used frequently but not meaningfully). In addition to spending nearly 20 years as an organizational consultant in London, I worked for four years as a government advisor in New Zealand. There, I witnessed one of the most incompetent change processes I could have dreamed of. This was run by one of the large global consulting companies. First, they had done little right but they thought they had done marvellously. Second, the change agents confused everyone every step of the way about whether or not they were creating real change or just cost savings (redundancy). Finally, at no stage did they speak 'plain English' but a version of gobbledygook.

It is rare to witness such change situations close up as a consultant, but I had these two experiences where I did. I had never witnessed anything like it. They were my impulse to start writing. They illustrate the issues many companies face when engaged in change processes. The book is not solely about mistakes, however. It is as much about what to do right. I learned about the latter from good consultants that I worked for and witnessed. Mostly they were from the fields of strategy and marketing or, at least, a million miles away from what I did, which was organizational behaviour and organization psychology. A few were in the same field as myself, like Professor Ed Schein and Professor Richard Beckhard, both from MIT, and both of whom taught me to consult.

My previous book, *Roles of Organization Development* (2015), set out and explored what roles to play to get consulting 'right'. In this book, I extend these ideas mostly in the direction of the concept of living systems. For me, this is encapsulated in the idea of creating human systems rather than engineering systems (see Chapter 5). All of the prescriptions offered in this book are those of a human system, up against the notions that embody engineering systems. Many consultants, such as in the two main case studies in this book, talk a good game about the human systems they are implementing but they don't add up. They are implementing engineering systems, and that is the heart of the problem with their change efforts.

One of the telltale signs of the latter is the need in the change team to fire people as a means of effecting change. For example, in case study A, my primary contact was the marketing manager. He was the effective managing director (not the formally appointed one). He wanted to bring a very old-fashioned company into the modern world. His aims were worthy and he had some backing from the other managers and, to some extent, the staff. However, it was a hard consulting assignment on my part. This was because of the degree to which he was self-deceiving, not self-aware (the first deadly sin).

He had the intelligence to be on top of all the reasons why the company should change and astute enough to be aware of what the company should be like instead. However, he kidded himself over how much in favour of these changes the rest of the company was. A self-aware person would, instead, know that he was asking a lot and know what he was asking intellectually and emotionally of the staff.

Instead of a straightforward assignment of change, I was tied to one that required me to forever be explaining reality to him. This meant we progressed much more slowly than we might otherwise have done. As an example, he, being frustrated, once called me in to a meeting with him to witness a long list of names, from which I was to advise him who should be fired and who should remain in the company. This was his method of getting change in the company. People who are prone to self-deception, kidding themselves, often end up wanting to fire people who don't get along with them, or are at odds with them in some way in order to accelerate the speed of change. People who are self-aware are busy building up other people and co-exist with people with whom they are at odds.

These themes are reflected in the chapters in the book.

Part I: Making the organization worse

Chapter 1: Self-deception and self-awareness

This chapter looks at instances of organizational change where the managers and consultants kid themselves about what is going on in the change effort. They kid themselves about the dynamic of the change programme and its worth. They miss obvious cues, especially any that would tell them they are off-track. They ignore the carefully blanked-out faces when the change effort is discussed. Communication exercises receive very few questions and the change team kid themselves over what that means. We look at signs when you are being **self-deceiving** (the first deadly sin). We look also at distinguishing between the change team's agenda and the organization's agenda (they are not the same). In contrast, a model to help with self-awareness is described. The first deadly sin is self-deception.

Chapter 2: The destruction of the identity of the organization

This chapter looks at how senior managers and especially external consultants can assume they are superior relative to the client company in general. The nature of their bias is explored in this chapter. The context is the identity of the organization, compared with the identity of the consulting company. The **arrogance and assumed superiority** of the change agents leads them to make decisions that, deliberately or inadvertently, propel them to change the identity of the organization. Sometimes the organization doesn't want or need this. Whether or not it does, this process leads to fireworks. One recipe to overcome this deadly sin (arrogance) is for the consulting team to analyse themselves in the same way that they normally analyse the client. (This keeps them honest.) I use knowledge of a psychological theory to help address the typical arrogance in the consulting team and change team. It is this arrogance which is the second deadly sin.

Chapter 3: Destroying cohesion in the organization

This chapter looks at maintaining and destroying cohesion in the organization. When the **interconnectedness is broken** (the third deadly sin), it takes a long time to fix it, by which time the consultants have gone and internal managers have to build back the cohesion. If you have a Holy War left in your organization between different divisions after the consultants have left, which wasn't there before, look to the lack of cohesion cultivated during the change effort. Cohesion doesn't mean elements in the organization are the same but includes the idea that different kinds of elements unite or cohere. We look at differentiation and integration and the importance of cultivating integrating roles, systems and structures. I describe a framework to work with the 'soft stuff', something which is not normally being done if the cohesion is being destroyed.

Part II: Making the organization better

Chapter 4: Gobbledygook

This chapter looks at gobbledygook and buzz words (the fourth deadly sin) and compares them with the right words. We look at the difference between processing information in terms of meaning and in terms of structure.

Gobbledygook is meaningless, by definition, and prevents change from succeeding. However, the use of gobbledygook and buzz words is rife on change projects, as is the cult-like behaviour that typifies them. We look at some transcripts from one of the case studies which illustrate how the use of buzz words could impact the change process. We look at social accounting: being responsible for the receivers of a piece of information hearing it as it was meant to be heard. We look also at creating communication for a specific emotional state rather than focusing only on the information you are conveying.

Chapter 5: Behaviour, not just strategy and structure

This chapter looks at the sleight of hand that occurs during a change process when behavioural change is glossed over (the fifth deadly sin). Many organizations conclude, wrongly, that behaviour change will occur if they only change the structure or systems or strategy. It will not. Trying to do so is what I refer to as '**pure lying**'. This occurs also when change efforts are labelled 'transformation' even though they only encompass cost savings and redundancy. We explore several mini case studies of behaviour change. We explore the idea of living systems and self-organizing as a principle in a change effort.

Chapter 6: Is the organization better, indifferent or worse?

How do you know? How can you tell? Is the organization better as a result of the change effort or have you just re-arranged the deck chairs on the Titanic? This chapter looks at how the measures of the change process can lead to a distorted measurement of change and the organization has, in fact, got **worse** (the sixth deadly sin). This chapter sets out a different model which enables you to work out whether you are wasting time, going backwards or achieving your change goals. This is related to the assumptions you have about what change looks like.

Part III: Resistance and reactions

Chapter 7: Resistance from intelligent people

Resistance of employees only occurs when intelligent people are given no view of the proceedings and aren't included in general in the change effort. We need to go beyond the idea that you 'overcome' resistance in employees. We need to re-focus on IQ as well as EQ. In other words, we need to assume that employees use their brains as well as hearts. Resistance comes from a practice of being **dictatorial** (the seventh deadly sin), not mutual. A new stance is to focus on how change agents act in such a way that resistance is created in employees and managers. Resistance occurs with intelligent dissenting adults who care about the organization and understand quite a lot about the nature of change. They are neither ignorant nor uncaring.

Chapter 8: The deep trauma of redundancy

This chapter explores ideas about redundancy and the reality of it in one organization. It explores the depth of **cruelty** in the change agents (the eighth deadly sin) and the depth of trauma in those affected. Most change efforts have not the slightest clue about the trauma of redundancy. We look at the difference between formal contracts and psychological contracts to explain it. The magnitude of the redundancy response is explained by seeing it as a rite of passage.

In summary, the book and its themes is illustrated in the table below.

Table 0.1 The eight deadly sins of organizational change and their opposite blessings

	Eight deadly sins of organizational change	*Eight opposite blessings of organizational change:*
Chapter 1	Self-deceptive	Self-aware
Chapter 2	Arrogance	Equal but different
Chapter 3	Destructive	Cohesive
Chapter 4	Gobbledygook	Meaning
Chapter 5	Focus on structure	Focus on behaviour and attitude
Chapter 6	Worse	Better
Chapter 7	Dictatorial	Mutual
Chapter 8	Cruel	Decent

Part I

Making the organization worse

1 Self-deception and self-awareness

Lying to yourself

> A survey of university professors found that 94% thought they were better at their jobs than their average colleague. . . . [Further, a] survey of one million high school seniors found that **all** students thought they were above average in their ability to get along with others . . . and 25% thought they were in the top 15.
>
> (Mele, 2001, p. 1)

Self-deception, the province of this chapter and the first deadly sin, is about lying to yourself rather than lying to others. Like the university professors and high school seniors, most of us do this to some extent some of the time. Self-deception simply means you are kidding yourself. This is often apparent to others more than it is to you. Self-deception in an organization can take over the whole change team, as we shall see in the case study shortly. It is not an ephemeral event but has serious consequences for the success of the change programme. Anything can be happening and you don't know it.

No longer in reality

In the conversations I had with people in one of my two main case studies (case study A), I realized more and more that the people in front of me were no longer talking reality. There was a conversation with one manager, who used to be in charge of the insurance business in the company. He was no longer in charge of his intellect or his senses. He was associated with the change team, run by a team of external consultants from one of the larger consulting companies. He had absorbed a lot of their change talk. However, he was, at heart, a down-to-earth likeable person. I wondered about the pressures on him to appear to toe the line in the change programme. I wondered, in short, about the extent to which the people around him were living in an unreal world.

The only problem, from my point of view, was that half the time I did not know what on earth he was talking about. Nor, when he started talking about applying his version of notions of chaos to the organization did I admit that I disagreed with him. I nodded politely and he kept on talking. This kind of dynamic was general across the organization (when interacting with the change team). The change team were trying to inflict an experiment on the organization. The rest of us were avoiding dealing with this fact. We didn't want to appear stupid or unknowing so we went along with their madness. With their kidding themselves.

In this chapter, this is what we explore: moments of kidding yourself during change that leads to unhelpful effects on the live human beings who work there.

Lying to yourself and lying to others

As Figure 1.1 shows, when you are kidding yourself you will be 'self-deceiving' if you are not also kidding others. If you are both kidding yourself as well as others then you 'haven't a clue'. You are naïve in this position. However, if you are not kidding yourself or others you are 'self-aware'. You are 'manipulative' when you are high in kidding others but not in kidding yourself. Others might put 'self-deception' where a person is kidding both themselves and high in kidding others. In what follows in this chapter, I have

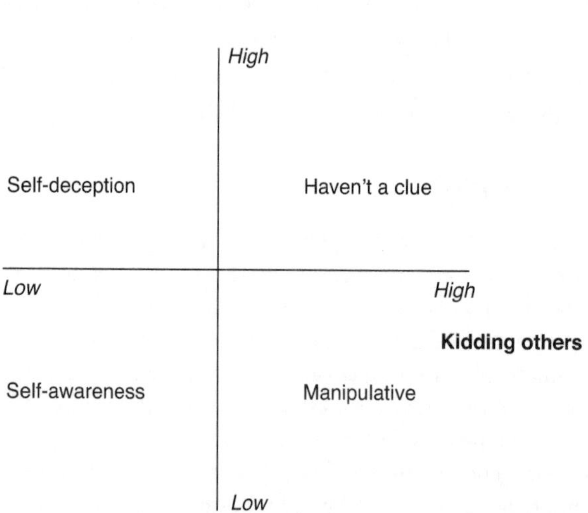

Figure 1.1 Kidding yourself and kidding others

used the idea of self-deception as 'kidding yourself'. In the next chapter, we focus on 'kidding others'.

Key points in this chapter

The key points in this chapter are set out below. We begin with some excerpts from a case study; one of two main cases running through the book. The first one is a finance company in the UK. This leads to some frameworks which aid us in avoiding self-deception and raising self-awareness.

- Self-deception: kidding ourselves
- The events in the change programme that shouldn't have occurred – case study A
- You don't observe in the first place
- You don't interpret meaning in events
- You don't know what you don't know
- Try to prove the opposite
- How can you tell if you are self-deceiving
- The change team has its own agenda
- A different model: self-awareness
- Ten questions
- Checklists

Case study A

What I have observed about change processes is that most organizations do not know what they are doing and most senior managers do not have a clue when it comes to change management. It is because of the latter that they hire one of the large consulting companies to make sure it 'goes well'. Both sets of people often lie to themselves or others about what is going on or should be going on. The case study illustrates the point.

Self-deception is a frequent occurrence with change programmes. It occurs because there is pressure to achieve, the change team is in the spotlight, people want to feel good about the change, and so on. This pressure to self-deception certainly existed in the following company.

A birds-eye view of a change programme that went strangely wrong[1]

During the time of the change programme, I had a birds-eye view of the series of events that unfolded during a period of about a year, when the finance company hired a large consulting company to conduct a large-scale change and transformation programme. In what follows I try to illustrate why the programme was derailed and why the consulting team was eventually fired by the board.

The excerpt that you see is the first part of the case study which we revisit in later chapters.

The team's mission was focussed on the client's strategy, structure, systems, skills and culture. The overall objective was to acquire greater flexibility to be able to respond to opportunities in the market place. They were faced with increasing competition and could anticipate a more difficult trading environment. The company was medium-sized and had been very successful for many years. In the past, they had ignored the management fads in the industry and had taken their own independent stance on many issues. However, they could also be rigid and certainly needed greater flexibility.

The change team had a sponsoring committee of three senior managers, who had formal responsibility for the project, reporting to the company's main board. The team doing the work were a mix of both internal managers from the company itself as well as the team of external consultants, who led the project.

The key events that arose that shouldn't have

During the year the consulting company was present, the company was effectively taken over by the programme. In terms of structure and decisions, as well as ongoing business activity, the project effectively became another 'organization' inside the client organization. The consulting team had decisive roles within the company, with little accountability to match their actual power. This kind of occurrence, in which a consulting team embarked on a large-scale programme is basically 'running' the company that hired them, is relatively frequent in organizations. Certainly, it was a major feature of this company during the time of the project, yet this fact was neither discussed nor noticed at board level nor by most of the senior management committee. This is not to suggest that it was a case of their knowing about the situation and sanctioning it. On the contrary. Consider why this very important fact went unnoticed.

Why people didn't have a clue

The fact that the change team were virtually running the company itself only went unnoticed because the programme itself had never been formally allocated such authority. However, the signs that they were actually doing so were highly visible, and the evidence was unmistakeable, in front of everyone's eyes and ears. Decisions would be referred to the project team, or delayed until they had made their reports. Members of the programme were present on major committees. Their work dictated what other work proceeded, and so on. Yet people failed to register these signs because they were composed of so many minutiae, of things that happened bit by bit every day, as well as because the team's actual power and scope had never been formalized by being sanctioned on a piece of paper. The perceptual scanners in this company seem to have been put out of action.

An innocent child would have easily noticed what was going on

Most people in the company were very cynical and even hostile towards the change programme itself as well as towards the consulting team. This was in spite of the fact that the general mood towards change was quite positive. This negative reaction was palpable as you walked around any of the company's buildings. It was reflected in the carefully blanked out faces when any discussion of the project occurred with the consulting team present. It was revealed by the lack of enthusiasm in the company as a general rule during this time, and in a myriad of other signs that would have taken an innocent child less than an hour to figure out. Yet the sponsoring group, plus the change team, were oblivious to all of this.

Communication exercises evoked no real questions or dialogue but this fact went unnoticed too

'Communication exercises' were specified as part of the consulting team's action plan. The aim of such exercises was to explain what the project was about, but they did so in broad outline only, and conveyed primarily the timings of the phases of the project. These exercises were meant to serve as a way for questions to be raised and subjects to be aired, but those that were brought into the open in this manner were trivial and different from the ones people discussed in other, less public, places. The fact that serious discussion never took place and that no challenging questions arose was accepted by the sponsoring committee and project team. This was because they weren't aware of the lack of such dialogue and because they never registered the significance of its absence. Yet it was obvious that questions and real debate should have occurred merely because it was such an important project. Their absence was a red warning. The team, however, heard only what was actually spoken instead of what was unspoken. But why? If, for example, they had been suggesting a radical new programme of events at a sports club, involving changes in structure and processes, and no questions were raised, they would think something was up. They would know they had to probe and find out what was really going on. In this company, however, as occurs in many other organizations, the change team saw and heard only the superficial things, the polite behaviour, the 'innocent' questions, the formal presentation, without applying their normal everyday common sense. Had the team possessed this, they would have 'heard' the fact that something that should have been said had failed to be said and they would have known what that meant.

They don't know what they don't know

The consulting team in case study A are kidding themselves. They are so self-deceiving that not only do they not know what they don't know but they don't know that they don't know that they don't know. They live in a time and space warp so extreme that even the obvious things are not seen or registered. Probably they are like this in all organizations they go to.

Is it possible to get out of it? To some extent. I once worked with a client on a consulting assignment for five years. He was high in self-deception but what he learned was three things:

1 He learned he didn't know that he didn't know
2 He learned to ask me and others questions to fill the gap
3 He learned that he usually didn't have the data for the conclusions he drew and knew he needed to sometimes 'pull back' from his normally go-getting style occasionally

The MD's secret assignment

The managing director, on the other hand, did know that there were things he didn't know. About eight months into the programme, he asked me for a meeting. He told me he had a secret assignment that no one was to know what he was going to ask me and I was not to tell anyone anything about my answers. He told me to go away and consider the questions for a week, and then go back to him. There were several questions and one that related to the change programme. He simply wanted to know what was going on. When I went back, I told him what I knew in answer to the questions. This involved personal comments on several senior managers. In addition, I told him about the dynamic in the organization that arose from the change programme, the angst and toxicity.

The consulting change team was so wrapped up in their own world that they could not predict that shortly over the next few months they would be fired. Table 1.1 sets out some examples of signs the consulting/change team should have noticed. Alongside each sign is their equivalent excuse or self-deception that can be inferred from their behaviour.

Table 1.1 Kidding themselves

Key signs they should have seen	*Excuses/self-deception*
• The organization was taken over by the project	• "The change programme is essential to our business"
• They didn't realize they had been taken over	• "I'm too busy to sit back and notice"
• Their perceptual scanners are out of action	• "We are simply getting on with it"
• Communications exercises are white-wash affairs	• "They should have asked questions; we can't ask them for them"
• No real dialogue anywhere	• "They are acting like children"
• Cult-like behaviour	• "We like being part of a group"

We need to be 'on top of these things'

Seeing and hearing are part of the human aspects of organizations. However, in organizations we focus on measuring formal things, e.g., budgets, sales. These are the technical aspects of organizations. We might measure engagement and motivation but these have nothing to do with the skills of avoiding self-deception. An attribute that is more closely associated with the latter is common sense. The consulting company in the case we have just looked at does not have much of this. They measured the formal things but not the informal things. Further, they hardly noticed anything.

They have no data for the conclusions they make

Self-deception is allied with the common occurrence of behaviour which has insufficient data for the conclusions that are made. This phenomenon has to be a mainstay of organizational life. People jump to conclusions more often than they actively find data that will lead to a conclusion. They may adopt a conclusion from someone else without checking it out, for example. They may presume that they already know the answer. Whatever the dynamic, it is rare to find people who have sufficient data for a particular conclusion. In a change programme, such behaviour is critical.

Why self-deception?

Where does such self-deception come from? To some extent the rest of the chapters answer that question:

- Arrogance and assumed superiority (Chapter 2)
- They don't want to acknowledge that cohesion is being destroyed (Chapter 3)

- They are too busy talking gobbledygook (Chapter 4)
- They don't want to focus on behaviour (Chapter 5)
- They don't want to face up to the fact the organization is getting worse (Chapter 6)
- They can't be seriously bothered with resistance (Chapter 7)
- They don't want to begin to consider the deep trauma of redundancy (Chapter 8)

Change team's agenda and the organization's agenda

There are at least two agendas to consider in any change programme: the organization's and the change team's. They are not the same thing (see Figure 1.2). Sometimes they are at variance. For example, the case study illustrates the situation where it is the change team's agenda that is being met not the organization's. Only if both the organization's and consulting team's agenda are met will you have a situation of 'everyone making sure it works'. When neither agenda is met, it is all a 'waste of time'. When the organization's agenda is met but not the consulting team's, the latter will simply 'go through the motions' of doing your programme and wait for or seek the next contract.

Contrasting companies

Two clients of mine provide contrasting examples of having a change agenda different or similar to the organization's agenda. In one large

Figure 1.2 The change team has its own agenda

company, they did not hire a large consulting company in but a group of three networked consultants (including myself). The other company hired one of the larger consulting companies. In both companies, the organization's agenda was for change in the organization. However, in the former the change team's agenda mirrored that of the organization's. In the latter, they were distinct. The change effort worked very easily and well in the former and was a disaster in the second. The key was to monitor the agenda of the organization and insist that the relevant consultants met it, not their own agenda.

You can increase self-awareness by using the idea of disproving hypotheses to get at the truth. You can write down some of your hypotheses or conclusions about the change process as well as the data that you think proves your conclusion. Then try to prove the opposite of your conclusion. For example, if your conclusion is that 'everyone is going along with the change', reverse this statement to 'hardly anyone is really going along with the change'. Now try to find the data, cues, information that proves the latter is true. This reverse process is designed to force you to get at the truth and increase your self-awareness. Once you have figured it out both ways, you can look at your reasoning, both conclusions and use common sense to discern where you think the truth actually is.

How can you tell if you are being self-deceiving?

It is hard to get change teams out of self-deception because they are riding high on it all. They want the messianic feeling of change. They can't see or hear the common sense. If you aren't doing the same thing, you are 'resisting'.

Here are some signs to use to figure out if you are self-deceiving.

- Do you keep smiling when the other person isn't?
- You are rigidly rational; so rigid you are told you are irrational
- Everything is always UP
- You think the recipients of the change are pleased with you
- You think of redundancies in a straightforward way
- You think there are no arguments against the change programme/process
- You believe 100% in the change effort.
- You think everyone else should be 100% also

- You ignore your own calculating attitude that makes you in favour of the change effort
- You think that if there are no questions or arguments against the change this is a positive sign

Self-awareness

One way to move to self-awareness is through an adaptation of Will Schutz's model of Truth, Choice and Self-regard (Schutz, 1984).

One framework is depicted in Table 1.2. The first step is to try to gauge what 'the truth' is in any particular situation. While everyone will have a different view of a situation, you can try to decipher a wider truth. This, in itself, will encourage self-awareness. Second, examine the situation with the following mind-set: Everybody is responsible and no one is to blame. One of the greatest obstacles to making progress in any situation is to start blaming. Third and finally, examine critically your level of self-knowledge and self-awareness in this situation. Is it high or low? Before taking action, it is essential to raise your level of knowledge and self-awareness.

Ask others to create a checklist

One way to get the data you are missing even if you have no idea what that data is, is to ask others to construct a checklist or questionnaire made up by those others, not you. Then get the checklists sent around to interested parties to fill in. You need to find out what you don't know and to some extent why you don't know it. My checklists for you are below in Checklists 1.1 to 1.3. They include a checklist on yourself, a checklist to be done on the change team and one for the senior management team. Comparable checklists are at the end of each chapter. Before these is a set of 10 questions you can ask yourself to better understand self-deception and self-awareness.

Table 1.2 Truth, no blame and self-awareness

Truth	*No blame*	*Self-awareness*
What is the truth in this situation	Everyone is responsible and no one is to blame	What level of self-awareness do you have in this situation

Ten questions about self-awareness and self-deception

1 In what way does a change situation in your organization mimic the case study?

....

....

2 What are the predominant forms of self-deception in your organization?

....

....

3 Does it even matter that the change team/programme is lying to themselves?

....

....

4 Describe what it means to see beyond the obvious

....

....

5 Are people usually aware that they are kidding themselves? If so, why do they do it? If not, how can you make them aware?

....

....

6 Can you discern the difference between the organization's agenda and the change team's agenda during a change effort?

....

....

7 In what way do people in your organization draw conclusions from insufficient data?

....

....

8 Can you turn ideas into their opposite? If so, describe the process

....

....

9 How can use the Truth, No-blame, Self-awareness model in your organization?

....

....

10 In general, how can you stop self-deception and increase self-awareness?

....

....

Checklist 1.1 On yourself

This is a checklist of 10 questions for others to answer about **yourself** to gauge your self-deception and self-awareness. Feel free to copy the checklist and use. Distribute to a minimum of 10 people. The context is any change programme you or your organization as a whole are engaged in.

	1 *Minimal*	*2*	*3*	*4* *Average*	*5*	*6*	*7* *Brilliant*
1 Am I self-aware and not kidding myself in general?							
2 Do I have good perceptual antennae?							
3 Do I have common sense?							
4 Do I understand the meaning in odd events?							
5 Can I see the difference between the change team's agenda and the organization's agenda?							
6 Do I know when others are kidding themselves?							
7 Do I tell the truth and know what it is?							
8 Do I know when I do not know?							
9 Do I find out what I do not know?							
10 Do I have a no-blame approach?							

Checklist 1.2 On the change team

This is a checklist of 10 questions for others to answer about the **change team** to gauge self-deception and self-awareness. Feel free to copy the checklist and use. Distribute to a minimum of 20 people. The context is any change programme they or your organization is engaged in.

	1	*2*	*3*	*4*	*5*	*6*	*7*
	Minimal			*Average*			*Brilliant*
1 Is the change team self-aware and not kidding themselves in general?							
2 Does the change team have good perceptual antennae?							
3 Does the change team have common sense?							
4 Does the change team understand the meaning in odd events?							
5 Does the change team know the difference between the change team's agenda and the organization's agenda?							
6 Does the change team know when others are kidding themselves?							
7 Does the change team tell the truth and know what it is?							
8 Does the change team know when they don't know?							
9 Does the change team find out what they don't know?							
10 Does the change team have a no-blame approach?							

Checklist 1.3 On the senior management team

This is a list of 10 questions for others to answer about the **senior management team** to gauge self-deception and self-awareness. Feel free to copy the checklist and use. Distribute to a minimum of 20 people. The context is the change programme they or your organization is engaged in.

	1	*2*	*3*	*4*	*5*	*6*	*7*
	Minimal			*Average*			*Brilliant*
1 Is the senior management team self-aware and not kidding themselves in general?							
2 Does the senior management team have good perceptual antennae?							
3 Does the senior management team have common sense?							
4 Does the senior management team understand the meaning in odd events?							
5 Does the senior management team know the difference between the change team's agenda and the organization's agenda?							
6 Does the senior management team know when others are kidding themselves?							
7 Does the senior management team tell the truth and know what it is?							
8 Does the senior management team know when they do not know?							
9 Does the senior management team find out what they do not know?							
10 Does the senior management team have a no-blame approach?							

Note

1 This cased is adapted from one appearing in Garden (2000).

2 The destruction of the identity of the organization

The arrogance of the change team

In this chapter we move from exploring self-deception to looking at the destruction of the identity of the organization and how this is related to arrogance and assumed superiority (the second deadly sin) of the change team in general and the consultants in particular. Here, the company (and the consultants) are just as effective at destroying the identity of the company as they were at kidding themselves. The arrogance first and foremost is related to an assumption of superiority by the consultants. However, there is a very strange dynamic that arises in change teams and that is the rapid spread of the arrogance disease to the whole of the change team – which often includes in-house employees – as they all become swept up with the excitement of the change effort. They start by being subtly rude to their colleagues who haven't made it onto the change team when they seek information from them.

I have always been fascinated by the creeping arrogance that exists on change teams. In one organization, the change leader from one of the large consulting companies was arrogance incarnate; boasting always, name dropping, referring to a person in another client by name. It was an unreal human performance. In another organization, I had to ring and ask one of the communications people on the change team (she was an in-house employee – junior to me) for some help. Her arrogance and rudeness were unsurpassed. She refused to answer my question and could barely bother to be civil. She was similar to the others on the change team. They were all impossibly arrogant. As soon as the internal recruits were put on the change team, they changed their nature and became too big for their boots.

What is arrogance composed of? The most user-friendly version is Berne's (1964) depiction of I'm OK you're Not OK. In each of the two case studies, there existed a team of external consultants combined with recruits from inside the organization. Instead of seeing their roles vis-à-vis those not in the change team, as equal but different, they universally reacted with arrogance. They tended to be despised more than admired by their colleagues. In one organization, where I was an employee for four years, I had two reactions to this procession of arrogance. One was that I was challenged and wanted to be on the change team where things were happening rather than being put on hold. The second was the utmost relief that I was not on the change team, having to adopt groupie behaviours and to mimic objectives I didn't agree with. They had adopted procedures which left human processes in their wake.

Lying to others

Chapter 1 was devoted to lying to yourself; self-deception. Chapter 2 is more focused on what happens when you lie to others or try to kid them. The change team cannot tell the truth if they are assuming superiority. They are lying to others if they misrepresent the truth of the situation.

Figure 2.1 illustrates.

Key points in this chapter

- Arrogance in the change team
- Misfit between the consulting company and the client
- Focus on the 'what' and the 'how,' not on the 'who'
- Focus on the identity of the company but not on that of the consultants
- Client is seen as wrong, not as different or unique
- Arrogance and assumed superiority of the change team and the consultants
- The consultants don't know they are trying to install a new identity
- The client's identity was to be individual; the consultants' was to be like others
- It is possible to alter the technical things in the company without killing off the 'who' of the organization, if you have a mind to
- Using the Myers Briggs Type Indicator (MBTI)
- How to stop acting so superior as a change agent
- Ten questions
- Checklists

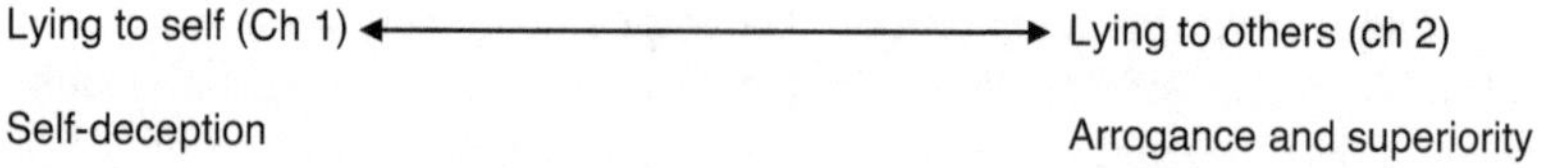

Lying to self (Ch 1) ⟵	⟶ Lying to others (ch 2)
Self-deception	Arrogance and superiority

Figure 2.1 Lying to self and to others

Another look at the finance company

As we will discover, there was a profound misfit between the client and the consulting team in terms of identity. This mattered extremely because of the arrogance and assumed superiority of the consulting company. In previous writing (Garden, 2000), I have called the 'identity' the psychological nature of the organization. Here I simply use the term 'identity'. It is allied to the 'who' of the organization and is not the same as 'culture'.

Case study A: Being at odds with the consultants you've hired

One of the most important factors that affected every aspect of the events that unfolded in the change programme with case study A, the finance company, was that the consulting team was at odds with the client in terms of 'who' it was. The focus of everyone's attention was, instead, on the decisions that needed to be made, on the reporting structures and what was to be delivered and by when. Everyone focused on the 'what' of the organization or the 'how' of the procedures, but nobody focused on the 'who' of the company or the programme team. Yet it was the profound misfit between the nature of the two that underlay a lot of what went wrong and which eventually railroaded the project. Note that the consulting team did think about the 'culture' of the company. They set out lists of what the culture of the company was, and what it 'should' be. But this has little to do with the identity of the company.

The consulting team saw the client as 'wrong' rather than as merely different and unique

The change team's approach ignored two key things. First, their approach looked only at the company and avoided defining the nature of the consulting team in the same way. Yet taking the latter course would have revealed true awareness on the part of the change team. This requires taking into account who you are as a change agent and the impact of that in relation to the company.

Second, instead of seeing the nature of the company as 'different', the consulting team saw it as 'wrong'. The team made no allowance for the possibility that their own assumptions about themselves and their client, or their implicitly held belief that their 'way' or nature was better, might affect their view of what needed to be done with the company. On the contrary, they attached no importance whatsoever to such considerations. Yet it was undoubtedly the case that their assumptions influenced their analysis, their definitions, every item on their seemingly objective questionnaires, and every recommendation. This lack of insight pervaded everything they thought, did and decided, yet was unseen and unaccounted for.

This led the consulting team to make their most profound mistake

Because the change team ignored such factors, their actions had effects that went way beyond what they had anticipated. For example, one of the ramifications was that the team assumed incorrect objectives. The explicit objectives of the programme included the aim that they should recommend something 'radical'. This became the team's main reference point or criterion, the one they worked with on a day-to-day basis. However, this was interpreted by them as meaning an aim of 30%–50% redundancies. This was their main way of improving the organization since, to them, it was so clear that the company was 'wrong'. This was their interpretation of the word 'radical': removing people and outsourcing as many activities from the organization as possible. Yet the company had been very successful, and still was at the time of the project. The consulting team had never even thought in terms of finding new revenue sources for the business to explore, for example.

Let me illustrate this another way. The general tenor in the company became that of 'having' to fire people. In the programme team, working out who should be dismissed or 'let go' was a major aspect of their activities and deliberations from the beginning. A new human resources manager sought evidence that one manager was unable to keep up with the changes implied by the project and gave that information to those who would fire that person themselves, or who enabled this to happen. Needing to make people redundant in a project like this is hardly unexpected. Such a preoccupation with it, however, is peculiar. It tells you that there is 'something going on here', or it should do.

The board belatedly discover what the team is up to

In fact, neither the board nor the senior management of the company had any assumptions about a target level of redundancies or about outsourcing, and had assumed that the project would, in fact, investigate new sources of revenue. While most had assumed that there would be redundancies, they were surprised when they finally discovered just what the team had taken upon themselves to achieve. To the consultants, the client company was simply 'wrong', instead of having a quite distinctive style that had, in fact, been the very source of its success. The only 'problem' was that this particular uniqueness, the company's 'way', was different from the implicit style and assumptions of the consulting team.

The consultants are oblivious

In reality, the consultants were trying to install a new identity for the company but, because they were oblivious to such things, failed to recognize that this, in fact, was what they were doing. For example, the practices which they advocated the company should adopt were those that followed the trends in the finance industry generally. Since 'doing what everybody else did' was the consulting team's own style, they automatically assumed that the company's image and natural style should likewise be in keeping with others in the industry. To them, this meant keeping up to date, being 'modern'. The company certainly needed to be more up to date in its information and computer processing, but it needed nothing less than to be the same in identity, style and image as everyone else in that particular business. The fact that the company was distinctive and went its own way was seen by the consultants as being out of step or even 'backward', yet it was precisely the company's individualistic approach and image, its having a mind of its own and a panache, that was the primary appeal to customers in the first place. Customers may have wanted faster administrative processing of their orders, but they also wanted 'who' the organization already was.

It is perfectly possible to have an organization modernize its systems yet still retain its own unique spirit, its special sense of self, 'who' it is. Unfortunately, however, we have few ways of figuring out how to achieve this.

The consulting team is, once again, unaware

The consulting team is, once again, unaware of themselves (self-deception). Here they are, given masses of power, tinkering away with who the client is. They have no idea of the implications of what they steadfastly do. One of the main reasons this is the case is their arrogance, their sense of superiority over the client.

The big consulting companies tend to have a high 'priority on self' but low 'priority on others'. In other words, they override the organization and the organization's ways. Not all of this is necessary, as has been seen in the case analysis. A group of 'networked consultants' place a high priority on others as well as self. Why is this the case? They have low overheads so don't need a big bang approach. Arrogance is not seen as a 'good' in itself but rather the opposite. Finally, they are not so fixated with the CEO or senior executives so they reach further down into the organization.

What clients often want, however, is 'dutiful consultants'. Such consultants are rare. Doing everything the client wants may not be what the client ultimately wants. When there is low priority on anyone, 'no one knows what they are doing' or why (see Figure 2.2).

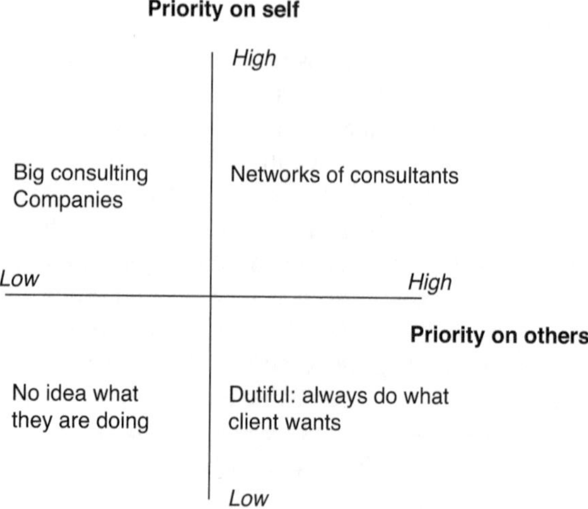

Figure 2.2 Priority on self or others

Insisting the consultants analyse themselves

I have seen these behaviours of arrogance, etc., in many change situations. They are always associated with the consultants not analysing themselves but only analysing the client. But that means the change won't work so well. It is self-defeating. It is possible to analyse yourself with standard personality questionnaires or with mapping strengths of the organizations with either qualitative assessments or quantitative ones.

Those change teams where arrogance is low and they are also analysing themselves are 'constructive' in their effects. As long as they are analysing themselves, even if they are arrogant they are not destructive: they simply 'don't take themselves so seriously'. When the change team is arrogant and they are not analysing themselves, we have a situation similar to case study A. When the change team is low in arrogance and low in analysing themselves, they will 'just get away with it'. Figure 2.3 illustrates.

The polarities set off by the style of the consultants

To understand the assumed superiority the consultants adopt we need to consider the change agents' style, or energy, not just the substance of what

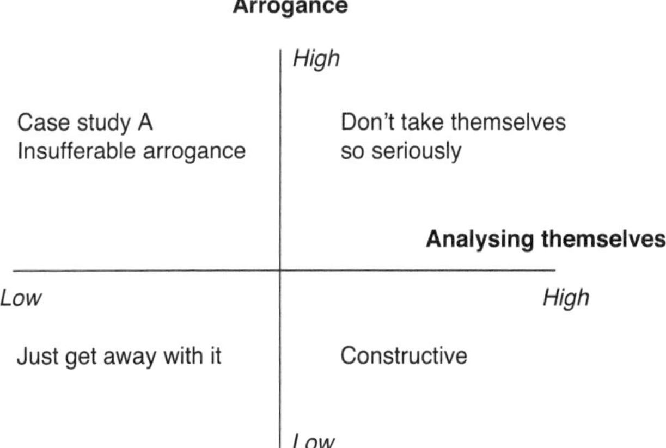

Figure 2.3 Arrogance and analysing themselves

Figure 2.4 Polarities in style of consultants

they do. It is often the overly charged style that is so off-putting to others on the receiving end. Recipients react by going in the opposite direction, as in Figure 2.4.

If the change agents' style is arrogant, one polarized response will be withdrawal (see Chapter 7). The latter is a frequent resistance reaction. The change agents become more arrogant as a result as they disdain a withdrawal response. Thus there is an unhealthy dynamic set up within the change process because of the original overweening arrogance.

How do you get out of it?

There is such a thing as the Law of Requisite Variety (Pascale et al., 2000, p. 20) which the consultants need to learn in relation to their self-analysis. This is

> an obscure but important law of cybernetics, [which] states that the survival of any system depends on its capacity to cultivate (not just tolerate) variety in its internal structure. Failure to do so will result in

an inability to cope successfully with variety when it is introduced from an external source.

Cultivating variety in its internal structure is the answer to arrogance and assumed superiority.

The Myers Briggs Type Indicator

The critical principle is to acknowledge that other people (or organizations) are *different* but that doesn't mean they are *wrong*, as in case study A. One tool I use in organizational change is the Myers Briggs Type Indicator (MBTI) (Myers et al., 2009). This can be used at the individual level as well as group level and organization level. It values differences in others as well as values you. Differences are not wrong but right.

The MBTI is a wonderful instrument to assess human personality. It follows from the theory of psychological types of Carl Jung (Jung, 1971). On reflection, Jung determined that there were different innate psychological types of people. The MBTI is a questionnaire which tries to gauge which personality type you are. You do not, however, need to actually use the questionnaire to discover your type. You can use reflection and observation instead.

There are four dichotomous dimensions in the MBTI.

1 Extraversion (E) and Introversion (I). These two opposites relate to how you orient yourself to people and take in energy.
2 Sensing (S) and Intuition (N). These two opposites relate to how you take in information.
3 Thinking (T) and Feeling (F). These two opposites relate to how you make decisions.
4 Judging (J) and Perceiving (P). These two opposites relate to how you deal with your outer world.

Table 2.1 Basic descriptors of the MBTI dimensions

Extraversion	Talking, making presentations, active, breadth, ebullience
Introversion	Reflection, making sure, independent, patience, depth
Sensing	Detail, practical, accurate, precision, carefulness
Intuition	Ingenious, overview, conceptual, imagination, speed, symbolic
Thinking	Logic, cut-and-dried, honest, analytical, objective
Feeling	People-oriented, values, considerate, friendly, appreciative
Judging	Order, timelines, sequential, measured, structured, steady
Perceiving	Adventurous, spontaneous, last-minute, risk-taker, enlivening

Thus, you end up on one side or the other of each of the four dimensions. They each have equal value. None is superior to any other.

How to stop being so 'superior' when you are a change agent

However, you *can* and are expected to develop your 'opposites'. Extraverts are supposed to value and develop the Introversion opposite pole (and vice versa). Intuitives are supposed to develop the opposite pole of Sensing (and vice versa). Feeling types are supposed to develop the opposite pole of Thinking (and vice versa). Judging types are supposed to develop the opposite pole of Perceiving (and vice versa). Some people do not like or value their 'opposite half' while the whole point of the MBTI theory is for you to value your opposite MBTI and value differences. But, often people don't do this. Sometimes this is because someone may see their own preferences as superior, not just as one half of an equally valued choice. This is what is going on with the external consultants and change teams where they view themselves as superior.

It is possible to detect that this has happened by considering the kinds of people who are devalued. This may be by criticizing certain kinds of people or not being able to tolerate them. Table 2.2 illustrates the kind of thing you may think of certain others.

For example, if you describe someone as sheepish, that means you are criticizing their Introversion. Or, if you can't stand isolated people, you may be devaluing Introversion. But we know that Introversion is equal in value to Extraversion, so we have detected an issue of lack of development of Introversion by that Extravert person criticizing. None of the signs of arrogance should occur. They indicate a problem with the person having these

Table 2.2 Signs of arrogance detected with the MBTI

MBTI orientation	*Misplaced criticism*
Extraversion	Boorish, hail-fellow-well-met, over-talks
Introversion	Sheepish, hides, fearful, too quiet, isolated
Sensing	Boring, stick-in-the-mud, unimaginative
Intuition	Gadfly, space cadet, off-the-wall
Thinking	Cold, hard, merciless
Feeling	Mushy, too-soft, flaky
Judging	Rigid, stuck, over-controlling
Perceiving	Chaotic, disorganized, adrenaline junkie

opinions. The table simply gives you a way of detecting what to watch out for in yourself and others. In other words, you will practice the Law of Requisite Variety.

A re-organization gone wrong

In one organization, I was asked to do a re-organization without necessarily making anyone redundant. The re-organization involved keeping various integrating structures as well as a restructuring. The issues in the organization were that they needed more flexibility to respond to new unpredictable demands from their environment. They were a professional services organization. They were highly intelligent and talented. They were organized into project teams.

My greatest obstacle, believe it or not, was the enthusiasm of the change team I worked with. They were very fired up to their task and worked out their own new structure independent of the one I was constructing. Their MBTI type was as follows: all Extravert, all Intuitive, all Thinking and all Perceiving (all ENTP). What they thought was a brilliant new structure was simply an ENTP structure. They hadn't analysed themselves or the effects of their type on their own work or their chosen design. However, it is impossible for a design suited to such a small group of people to work. Their ENTP version was a little akin to an engineering system, not a human system. It was very technically based. The known Feeling types in the organization had their own particular personal project structure decimated. The only problem with this new structure was that it didn't cater to half the employees; in particular to the Sensing types and Feeling types. The enthusiasm for this ad hoc design had been a waste of time. Unfortunately, the branch manager was also an ENTP and thought it was marvellous. My own design (which balanced the needs of Thinking and Feeling types) was seen as a massive challenge. This was because it legitimized the needs of feeling types. If the actual design does not do so, then you are likely to get suppressed resentment and dissatisfaction from the Feeling types who are trying to work in an alien organization. Change teams do the same when they do not analyse themselves: create an alien organization for some of the MBTI types. This is one of the reasons why it is critical for the change team to analyse themselves not just the organization.

Ten questions about arrogance and assuming superiority

1 Do you identify your organization with the finance company in case A?

....

....

2 If yes, in what way?

....

....

3 Instead of focusing on the 'what' and the 'how' of your organization, can you also include the 'who' of the organization?

....

....

4 What is the effect of arrogance and superiority assumptions in your organization?

....

....

5 Where is any arrogance and assumed superiority located in your organization?

....

....

6 How is this managed, or isn't it?

....

....

7 In your organization, are people allowed to be different or is that seen as wrong?

....

....

8 Have you ever been pressured to follow the line of others in your industry (follow a fad)?

....

....

9 If you relate the MBTI to your organization, how would you type it?

....

....

10 What are the overall signs to watch for to stop arrogance and superiority creeping in?

....

....

Checklist 2.1 On yourself

This is a checklist of 10 questions for others to answer about **yourself** to gauge arrogance and assumptions about superiority. Feel free to copy the checklist and use. Distribute to a minimum of 10 people. The context is any change programme you or your organization are engaged in.

	1	*2*	*3*	*4*	*5*	*6*	*7*
	Minimal			*Average*			*Brilliant*
1 Am I free of arrogance and assumptions of superiority?							
2 Can you tease me?							
3 Do you think I view others as equals?							
4 Do I make it a common practice to analyse myself and my biases?							
5 Do I appreciate the identity of the organization?							
6 Do I create an atmosphere which values others?							
7 Can other people be different around me?							
8 Can I treat the idiosyncrasies of other divisions with tolerance?							
9 Is it easy to tackle arrogance and assumed superiority around me?							
10 Am I attempting to alter the identity of the organization without realizing it?							

Checklist 2.2 On the change team

This is a checklist for others to answer about the **change team** to gauge arrogance and assumptions about superiority. Feel free to copy the checklist and use. Distribute to a minimum of 20 people. The context is any change programme the change team or your organization are engaged in.

	1	*2*	*3*	*4*	*5*	*6*	*7*
	Minimal			*Average*			*Brilliant*
1 Is the change team free of arrogance and assumptions of superiority?							
2 Can you tease them?							
3 Do you think they view others as equals?							
4 Does the change team make it a common practice to analyse themselves and their own biases?							
5 Do they appreciate the identity of the organization?							
6 Do they create an atmosphere which values others?							
7 Can other people be different around the change team?							
8 Can the change team treat the idiosyncrasies of other divisions with tolerance?							
9 Is it easy for the change team to tackle arrogance and assumed superiority?							
10 Is the change team attempting to alter the identity of the organization without realizing it?							

Checklist 2.3 On the senior management team

This is a checklist of 10 questions for others to answer about the **senior management team** to gauge arrogance and assumed superiority. Feel free to copy the checklist and use. Distribute to a minimum of 20 people. The context is any change programme they or the organization are engaged in.

	1 *Minimal*	*2*	*3*	*4* *Average*	*5*	*6*	*7* *Brilliant*
1 Are the senior management team free of arrogance and assumed superiority?							
2 Can you tease them?							
3 Do you think they view others as equals?							
4 Does the senior management team make it a common practice to analyse themselves and their own biases?							
5 Do they appreciate the identity of the organization?							
6 Do they create an atmosphere which values others?							
7 Can other people be different around the senior management team?							
8 Can the senior management team treat the idiosyncrasies of various divisions with tolerance?							
9 Is it easy for the senior management team to tackle arrogance and assumed superiority?							
10 Is the senior management team attempting to alter the identity of the organization without realizing it?							

3 Destroying cohesion in the organization

Living systems

Gallup's strength finder is a wonderful instrument for self-insight. I used it a year ago and came out with a list of five strengths. The intriguing one was called 'connectedness'. It meant that you believe that each thing/person is connected to every other thing/person across the world. This was my fourth highest 'strength'. I was fascinated. It is this rather airy-fairy idea that we explore in this chapter.

A similar viewpoint is expressed by the field of 'living systems'. A leading exponent of this field, Fritjof Capra (1996; Capra and Luigi, 2014) explains how we are transforming from a mechanistic worldview to one based on life sciences. Capra sees the world

> not as a collection of isolated objects; but as a network of phenomena that are fundamentally interconnected and interdependent. This paradigm recognises the intrinsic value of all living beings and views humans as just one particular strand in the web of life.
>
> (Capra, 1996, p. 7)

The living systems view reveals a particular relationship between the parts and the whole.

> The emphasis on the parts has been called mechanistic, reductionist, or atomistic; the emphasis on the whole holistic, organismic, or ecological . . . in [the] systems view, the essential properties of a . . . living system, are properties of the whole, which none of the parts have. They arise from the interactions and relationships among the parts. . . . The properties of the parts are not intrinsic properties but can be understood only within the context of the larger whole.
>
> (Capra, 1996, p. 29)

Further, Capra states, "the exploration of living systems – organisms, parts of organisms, and communities of organisms – had led scientists to the same new way of thinking in terms of *connectedness, relationships and context*" (Capra, 1996, p. 36, my italics).

This chapter relates to cohesion which is similar to the idea of being connected (Gallup) and an integrated whole with a priority on connectedness and relationships (Capra).

What is cohesion?

One year, I watched as one of the larger consulting companies destroyed the cohesion I had painstakingly built up in an organization as a consultant. The consultants had an organization-wide scheme to implement but they did not evoke organization-wide sentiments. On the contrary, managers and employees were bewildered and shrank back into compartments, their own groups. I was bewildered and didn't know what to say to employees I used to know. It was agonizing waiting to see what would happen to the consultants. I prayed they would be fired and have to leave this precious company alone. Sometimes it is better for the consultants to not have been employed at all.

The colloquial understanding of cohesion in organizations would mirror the themes mentioned already of being close or united, working in consort. However, for the most part cohesion in the academic literature relates to group cohesion whereas in this chapter we are focused on organizational cohesion. Note that I will not be talking only about different elements of the organization being the *same*. I mean also connection between *different* kinds of elements.

Cohesion is a mightily important and desirable phenomenon. It is linked to productivity and performance; poor performance is likely to result from low cohesion (and vice versa) and high performance is likely to result from high cohesion (and vice versa). Yet, as we shall see, it is treated as an unnecessary reality by change agents and consulting companies who tend to destroy the organization's cohesion or connectedness (the third deadly sin) as they continue their change programme.

In this chapter, we look again at case study A to illustrate the themes.

Key points in this chapter

- Gallup and Capra
- What is cohesion?
- Connections across the finance company were broken
- The change team did not seem to think they should have fixed the broken bits *during* the programme

- Soft stuff was outside their brief (to be carried out by internal managers)
- An organization was seen as a series of lines on a bit of paper
- A Holy War erupts within the organization
- They didn't have the skills to deal with the soft stuff anyway
- The purpose of integrating roles
- Inclusion, control and openness – a framework for the soft stuff

Let's look at what was happening in case study A, where the issue was that of destruction of cohesion in the company.

Case study A: The project unintentionally damages the connections in the company

One of the main consequences of the fact that the change team failed to fully account for the effects of what they were doing was that the invisible connections that had previously existed across the company were broken, yet the purpose of the programme should have been exactly the opposite.

One impetus behind the programme was to link the company's administrative and information processes from one end of the organization to the other. The change team were aware of the need for these aspects of the organization to be technically compatible, but there are other kinds of compatibility to consider as well. One is whether the processes will enhance the emotional connections that exist within the organization or whether they have the opposite effect. This other kind of interdependence was never considered by the change team, who thought that any damage to the cohesion of the company could be 'fixed' after the project could be carried out, by the internal managers still there. In that sense, they saw the need to maintain cohesion and a subtle interdependence as outside their brief, rather than as an intrinsic aspect of the change effort which they were responsible for from the beginning.

The team is oblivious to the fact that an organization is more than a series of lines on a chart

The change team had no idea that they needed to take responsibility for the fact that the company needed to be connected in these other, more subtle ways. They thought about the organization as a whole only in terms of its overall structure, the reporting lines, who was responsible for what, and as lines across the organization chart to work out what should go where. However, this is to think of the organization as merely a series of lines.

The idea of the company as a single connected thing was something to which the change team were oblivious. That is why they thought they could break it into pieces and put it back together again as if it were some kind of jigsaw. Consequently, by the end of the project, valuable aspects of the organization that had served to connect different parts together had been damaged.

Evoking a Holy War between certain divisions within the company

One disconnection that resulted was a split between certain parts of the company. Two divisions in the company withdrew increasingly from the change programme throughout the time the consultants were present. Mainly they objected to the change in nature that the programme implied and its effect upon 'who' they were (Chapter 2). They also thought that the project was damaging the trust and commitment within the company, which they saw as a key ingredient in their success. They resisted fiercely the attempts by the change team to break the foundations linking people and the connections that served to coordinate and smooth their day-to-day actions.

The cohesion is worse

As a result, one of the divisions explicitly banned the project from having any impact on them at all, and the other division delayed the programme from having any impact on them for a year. While it is true that, prior to the start of the programme, the first division had functioned as a separate department within the company, with its own laws and style, there had never been the kind of ugly Holy War, nor barricades erected to ward off the project team, that existed during the programme. There was less common understanding and interdependence after the programme had been in existence for a while than had been the case before the programme began, and less of a common footing for the organization to move forward with. The business changes the change team recommended could have been made quite successfully without any loss to their sense of well-being.

Fixing the company afterwards

This kind of connection (Capra) and compatibility is vital to the functioning of any organization. It is one of those things that we all know yet have few words with which to refer to it. As a result, it is treated as a kind of residual factor, something to be 'fixed' after the organization has done what is considered the 'real' work, like getting business processes changed or a strategy sorted out. But this connectedness can and should be included as an explicit part of the 'real' business at the same time as everything else, at the beginning. In addition, it should be treated as coming within the area of responsibility of the programme itself.

How can they not know?

How can the change team not know so much destruction of cohesion was occurring? They:

- Are not really aware of having destroyed cohesion
- Have no intention of fixing the issues
- Have no capability to fix the damage
- Think connectivity is to do with communication

The continuum from destruction to cohesion and vice versa

You can start at either end of the continuum of Figure 3.1. Change programmes usually start at the cohesion end and get slowly worse. This leads to discomfort and tension as the people in the organization decide that anything wrong should be fixed afterwards. It seems too difficult and widespread to deal with it now. At this point, things are still manageable, but if the tensions continue, the situation gets worse. Connections across the organization start to break. The situation at this point means it is harder to fix

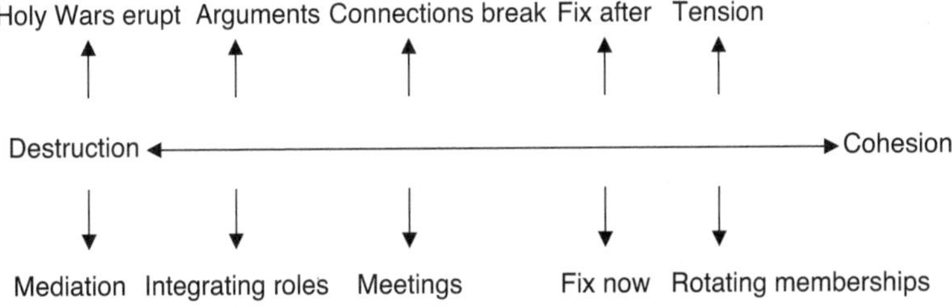

Figure 3.1 The continuum from destruction to cohesion

the damage to the cohesion. Arguments start to break out in earnest without the glue or bonding present as before. Destruction is when Holy Wars break out between different parts of the organization and certain units break off any real or meaningful contact with outsiders.

If you are travelling in the opposite direction, from destruction to cohesion, you need to start with mediation of the Holy Wars. If you can resolve these, you need integrating structures and roles where divisions involved in the Holy Wars have participation in the change team if they want it. This will resolve some of the arguments. You need to keep going with these. While this is happening, you can fix some of the connections that have been broken. This may take a long time. Instead of fixing it later, you fix it now. Tension between the units will partly resolve themselves with more rotating memberships.

Excuses to fix the cohesion afterwards

In general, change teams either assume that internal managers will fix the situation afterwards or insist that this destruction is temporary, inevitable or doesn't matter. If they knew, what excuses do they make to justify the fact that the cohesion is worse?

- "It is inevitable that cohesion will get worse temporarily"
- "We don't have time to deal with this"
- "Our real task is to fix the business"
- "We don't have any measures for this (cohesion)"
- "We are preoccupied with trying to get another contract"

None of these excuses is justified. Instead, we need a set of principles to guide the management of cohesion in the organization first because it is so important and second because it is so frequently damaged.

Five golden rules

- The change team is made **aware** of the cohesion issues
- The change team takes **responsibility** for cohesion issues
- The change team **does not assume** the internal managers will fix what the change team has done
- The change team has **tools** to understand and work with the cohesion issues
- The change team is made responsible for there being **no Holy Wars** emerging

Living systems or killing-off systems

A living system contrasts with the idea that the organization is a series of lines on a paper. The latter is a disembodied organization that replicates an engineering system, not a human system (Chapter 5). What we are dealing with is a human phenomenon, not a technical one. To Capra we are more than a human system but a living system. A part of a system is a "pattern in an inseparable web of relationships" (Capra, 1996, p. 37).

If this viewpoint is valid, organizations are more complicated and more simple than we usually assume. It is based on networks of relationships rather than a building or an organization structure.

Integrating roles and structures

There are two basic principles in organizing (one of which is particularly important in cohesion). One is differentiation and the other is integration. Differentiation means you divide things up, usually put like-roles together and create separate boundaries to unlike roles. Integration means you connect things across the organization. Good management requires you to both differentiate and integrate. If all you do is differentiate and not integrate, you will damage the cohesion. Further, you will create a never-ending round of re-structuring and re-structuring. There should be integrating structures in the organization chart and integrating processes.

An integrating role and person

The best example of an integrating role I have seen was in the public sector. It was a small organization, around 130 people. The client was a real hurdle. She was one of those managers who believed in re-drawing lines on a bit of paper to reflect the organization she wanted. The branch I was involved in was very successful and had quite motivated people. The interesting bit was that they had in the organization a pure integrating role at a senior level. How did it work?

There were about 50 different projects being worked on at different times in this organization, and the integrating person would float between these projects with about six projects being more intensively worked on by him than the other projects. No one told him what to do by when. He would detect by himself what needs existed on which projects and assign himself to them. The teams accepted him in this role. The role was sorely needed but the client was not comfortable because she saw it as unstable and therefore outside her differentiating, controlling mind-set. She should have been mature enough to build up the roles she was uncomfortable with. She wanted what was a brilliant integrating role to fit neatly into the differentiating lines on her organization chart, thereby destroying it.

Integrating approaches and roles on the change programme

- A variety of people is included on the change team
- There is a lot of rotation of people on the change team
- Integrating structures, roles and people are added to or retained
- The change team talks widely and deeply across the organization in spite of their time commitments

How do you ensure integration occurs and, thereby, the required cohesion in the organization? First and foremost, you need a variety of people on the change team. This means variety not just in technical or job terms but also in personality and style. Second, whomever you have on the change team, rotate them frequently in spite of the cost in terms of experience on the team. Remember the agenda is the organization's, not the change team's. When you rotate frequently you are giving more people the chance to be involved and more chance to lessen the friction with the wider organization. As a third principle, you need to find integrating roles and structures and protect them explicitly, in the deliberations of the change team and the actions and decisions of the organization. Last, to build on integration, the change team needs to talk widely and deeply in the organization. Many of the mistakes concerning integration stem from the change team talking to a narrow set of people.

Working with the soft stuff

How can you work easily with the soft stuff like cohesion? For example, in a Holy War, why is their existence seemingly threatened? How would you explain it? On the basis of personality, or politics? As spoilt children?

One framework I use to answer questions like this is that derived from Will Schutz (1984): Inclusion, Control, Openness. The original theory was social-psychological, specifying the different ways in which people interact with each other. My own adaptation of it (Garden, 2000) looks at the organization as a whole. It can be used to guide you through issues like cohesion.

A framework for the soft stuff

We have many ways of deciphering the business or marketing ramifications of the actions and decisions an organization takes but are often lost when trying to understand the invisible, emotional or cohesive stuff. The main benefit of a framework that provides a point of view to do the latter is to make those invisible things visible, the implicit explicit.

The Schutz theory states that three core areas of experience exist in any interaction between individuals, namely inclusion, control and openness. In relation to **individuals**, the inclusion area of experience describes the frequency and style of one's interaction with others, as well as how one establishes an identity alongside others. The control area of experience describes that area of experience related to exerting influence and establishing effectiveness. Openness describes that area of experience related to the manner of direct engagement with others and the way in which relationships are sustained.

The aims and activities of any **organization** can also be explained in terms of the same three areas of experience or three sets of needs. These areas are the same for individuals, groups, business areas, and the organization as a whole (see Schutz, 1984; Garden, 2000). I define them as set out below in Table 3.1.

Table 3.1 Three areas of experience for the organization

Inclusion aims	People are valued in themselves not just for doing a good job; people are able to express their individuality without being pressed into faddish behaviours; people interact freely; there is a unique individuality for that organization; people can claim time and attention when they want to; people feel their existence or way of doing things is not threatened; people's energy is usually up; the identity of the organization is clear
Control aims	to create a means of expressing the organization's power and talent so that people achieve what they set out to; you can influence others without being overbearing and adapt to others without being a pushover; people can maintain a feeling of being in control and on top of things; people have a clear direction to aim for; people are comfortable with competing as well as with the risk of change; there is a deep rather than superficial confidence
Openness aims	People believe in the organization; people have a manner of engaging with others that is real and genuine rather than superficial; they create relationships with others that can be sustained; people take care of themselves in a way that ensures well-being for the long term; people engage genuinely with tasks; there is a larger agenda that fulfils a sense of purpose and has meaning; there is loyalty and commitment; there is a high level of trust in the organization

Using the framework

Analysis of case study A

The main area of experience in the finance company (relevant to the change process) is the Openness aims. People stopped believing in their organization, and the level of trust plummeted. Peoples' relationships became false as the level of trust fell. People started acting selfishly, not to ensure their well-being for the long term. Stress levels skyrocketed. Loyalty to the whole company shrank as the change proceeded.

As far as the Inclusion area of experience is concerned, there are several areas of concern as well: First, the existence of a Holy War means that those parts of the organization felt their existence (or way of being) was threatened with annihilation – they wouldn't exist anymore. People were definitely not allowed to express their individuality anymore. This was mirrored in the organization not being able to express its clear identity anymore.

Regarding the Control area of experience: people did not express power and talent was blocked. Decisions were blocked so people were not able to achieve what they set out to; the change programme had taken over. People were not in control or on top of things. There was no clear direction and no confidence around competing.

The key benefit of a framework like this is to check whether your actions and interventions will make the organization better or worse. If the key area 'impacted' by the change programme is Inclusion, you need to address those issues with measures that could be characterized as Inclusion. If you do not, and use measures that can be characterized as Control or Openness, you will make the situation worse.

The aims you are working with are behavioural and sometimes psychological. The basic method is to describe the behaviours in each dimension. Then hone in on the most significant dimension as it seems to you. Finally, work out how you are going to deal with those issues. Note that cohesion relates to all three dimensions, not just openness.

You can use it to monitor the effect of any change programme and use it qualitatively or quantitatively. I have used it for 20 years and it never fails me. The detail is set out in the three pages following.

Table 3.2 Inclusion sphere of experience

Too little focus on Inclusion	*Healthy Inclusion*	*Too much focus on Inclusion*
Score 1, 2, 3	Score 4, 5, 6	Score 7, 8, 9
• Poor presence in the market • No clear idea of 'who' it is as an organization • Not able to easily claim space in the market or environment • Doesn't interact easily with other organizations • Too rigid in going its own way • Everyone too focused on being individuals rather than part of a group • Too reliant on innovation • Over-relies on quiet spaces (physical) • People do not communicate enough • People are valued only for the work they do, not in themselves	• Easily able to establish presence as an organization • Clear identity ('who' it is as an organization) • Interacts well with other organizations • Able to go its own way in its industry • Innovative • Balances the needs of individuals and groups • Uses appropriate participation • Very consultative • Balances doing work in groups and as individuals • Balances open planning with quiet spaces	• Always trying to get attention in the market or environment • Too participative • Relies too much on groups • Follows fads • Too entertaining • Always having to be up-to-date • Noisy • Stuck on me-too products • Spend too little on R&D • Overbearing • Massive open planning • People are always using jargon words • Need to be 'in' • Marketing and sales are king • People talk too much
Feelings • Excluded • Ignored • Annihilated • Invisible	**Feelings** • Got it 'together' • Even-keel • Noticed • Significant	**Feelings** • Swamped • Burnt-out • Scattered • Dismembered
Atmosphere • People feel deprived of attention • Exclusive clubs • Febrile • Opaque	**Atmosphere** • People are aware of their significance • Good mix of work and play • Presence • Good healthy energy	**Atmosphere** • Strung out • Over-do the playfulness • Focus on appearances • Childish

Table 3.3 Control sphere of experience

Too little Control	*Healthy Control*	*Too much Control*
Score 1, 2, 3	Score 4, 5, 6	Score 7, 8, 9
• Too flexible • Doesn't achieve goals • Too little structure • Doesn't like power • Talent is there but disorganized • Always changes plan even when not necessary • Relies on being very resourceful rather than acquiring assets • Doesn't beat the competition because people are always changing their mind • Doesn't believe in control mechanisms • Nobody knows what is going on • Information is scattered through the organization • Decisions are made loosely	• Effective at achieving goals • Comfortable with power • Has self-confidence without being macho • Easily releases talent • Can plan well and change plan instantly • Emphasizes reliability • Able to gain resources it needs to meet its goals • Competitive in industry • Adjusts control measures to suit what is going on in organization • Empowerment is real • Information is a resource • Decisions are made where the information is	• Rigid • Hierarchical • Bureaucratic • Abuses power • Macho boasts • Doesn't know how to release talent • Over-plans and clings to plan • Not resourceful • Too stodgy to beat competition • Relies on formal mechanisms to run organization • People are too governed by control mechanisms • Too much information (as it is seen as a means of control) • Decisions are made where the role in the hierarchy is
Feelings • Humiliated • Scared • Powerless • Helpless	**Feelings** • Competent • Able to cope • Useful • In control of self	**Feelings** • Stultifying • Abusive • Puffed up • Abrupt
Atmosphere • People do not use their potential • Feel wasted • People drop things • Having fun but . . .	**Atmosphere** • Glide along • Can deal with challenges • Can-do • Empowering	**Atmosphere** • Can't change • Avoid behaviour/soft stuff • Interrupt others • Boastful

Table 3.4 Openness sphere of experience

Too little Openness	*Healthy Openness*	*Too much Openness*
Score 1, 2, 3	Score 4, 5, 6	Score 7, 8, 9
• Not good at creating genuine relationships • Relationships are short term • Disloyal in organization • People don't believe in it • No enthusiasm • Don't engage genuinely with tasks • Don't try to fix problems • Impersonal • Don't evoke real commitment • People shy away from each other • Few personal friendships • Little loyalty from customers • People don't really like each other • Quite high staff turnover	• Creates genuine good relationships • Good at sustaining relationships over long term • Creates loyalty in and out of the organization • Easily able to get others to believe in it • Communicates enthusiasm for what it does • People engage genuinely with their tasks • People truly fix problems • Evokes a personal response from others • Customers are loyal to the organization • Take account of their effects on others • People like each other • Longevity	• Over-the-top relationships • People are disloyal in the organization • People just say they believe in it • False enthusiasm • People are too busy with relationships • Appear to do things • Overly personal, invasive • Not real or genuine • Customers are effusive but not loyal • Focus on fixing the relationship not the problem, but customers want them to fix the problem • Easily embarrassed • Friendly to you but don't like you • Quick turnover of staff
Feelings • Tight (uptight) • Cold • Pessimistic • Clinical	**Feelings** • Open • Warm • Optimistic • Personable	**Feelings** • Self-oriented • Egotistical • Exhausting • Time-wasters
Atmosphere • Professional • People focus only on work • Presentational • Clipped	**Atmosphere** • Friendly • People believe in ideals and values • Relaxed • Honest	**Atmosphere** • Artificial • People believe in their own agenda • Miss the point • Evasive

Ten questions on destroying the cohesion

1 How do you understand Capra's worldview?

....

....

2 Can you apply it to organizations?

....

....

3 Have you been through an experience in your organization of having the cohesion damaged?

....

....

4 If so, what happened?

....

....

5 How do you think cohesion can be increased in your organization?

....

....

6 Do you tend to think other people will 'fix the cohesion' afterwards?

....

....

7 Do people in your organization think of the organization as a series of lines on a piece of paper?

....

....

8 Do people have the skills to deal with the soft stuff in the organization?

....

....

9 Are they resistant or defensive in dealing with the soft stuff?

....

....

10 Relate the Inclusion, Control, Openness framework to your organization

....

....

Checklist 3.1 On yourself

This is a checklist of 10 questions for others to answer about **yourself** to gauge destruction and cohesion. Feel free to copy the checklist and use. Distribute to a minimum of 10 people. The context is any change programme you or your organization are engaged in.

	1 *Minimal*	*2*	*3*	*4* *Average*	*5*	*6*	*7* *Brilliant*
1 Am I good at creating cohesion?							
2 Do I understand an organization is not a series of lines on paper?							
3 Do I understand that the whole is more than the sum of its parts?							
4 Am I good at maintaining the subtle connections during change?							
5 If cohesion is destroyed, am I good at fixing it?							
6 Am I good at fixing it immediately, not waiting until afterwards?							
7 Do I avert Holy Wars?							
8 Am I good at dealing with the soft stuff in general?							
9 Do I value integrating roles in the organization?							
10 Do I help create integrating structures in the organization?							

Checklist 3.2 On the change team

This is a checklist of 10 questions for others to answer about the **change team** to gauge destruction and cohesion. Feel free to copy the checklist and use. Distribute to a minimum of 20 people. The context is any change programme they or your organization are engaged in.

	1	*2*	*3*	*4*	*5*	*6*	*7*
	Minimal			*Average*			*Brilliant*
1 Is the change team good at creating cohesion?							
2 Does the change team understand the organization is not a series of lines on paper?							
3 Does the change team understand that the whole is more than the sum of the parts?							
4 Is the change team good at maintaining the subtle connections during change?							
5 If cohesion is destroyed, is the change team good at fixing it?							
6 Is the change team good at fixing cohesion immediately, not waiting until afterwards?							
7 Does the change team avert Holy Wars?							
8 Is the change team good at dealing with the soft stuff, in general?							
9 Does the change team value integrating roles in the organization?							
10 Does the change team help create integrating structures in the organization?							

Checklist 3.3 On the senior management team

This is a checklist of 10 questions for others to answer about the **senior management** team to gauge destruction and cohesion. Feel free to copy the checklist and use. Distribute to a minimum of 20 people. The context is any change programme they or your organization are engaged in.

	1 *Minimal*	*2*	*3*	*4* *Average*	*5*	*6*	*7* *Brilliant*
1 Is the senior management team good at creating cohesion?							
2 Does the senior management team understand the organization is not a series of lines on paper?							
3 Does the senior management team understand that the whole is more than the sum of its parts?							
4 Is the senior management team good at maintaining the subtle connections during change?							
5 If cohesion is destroyed, is the senior management team good at fixing it?							
6 Is the senior management team good at fixing it immediately, not waiting until afterwards?							
7 Does the senior management team avert Holy Wars?							
8 Is the senior management team good at dealing with the soft stuff in general?							
9 Does the senior management team value integrating roles in the organization?							
10 Does the senior management team help create integrating structures in the organization?							

Part II

Making the organization better

4 Gobbledygook

Needing meaning in the finance company: case study A

Organizational change needs to be real, not full of empty buzz words. In the case I have been using so far, the financial services company, the change programme was full of gobbledygook and buzz words (the fourth deadly sin). Accompanying these was the inevitable cult-like behaviour.

At one point, I was invited to one of the meetings of the external consulting company. They wanted to pick my brains. I was associated with the sales division but knew all the executive committee well. There were about 12 people in the consulting group meeting. It was then that the fact that they were aiming for 30%–50% redundancies was stated. They met every week to have a supposedly no-holds barred meeting about the change programme. The team leader led the meeting. The reason I was there that day unfolded. The leader turned to me at one point and explained that they wanted me to tell them how to get around the dominant member of the Executive Committee because they couldn't. I uttered some inanities in reply because I had no intention of telling them how to get around anything.

The main problem was that the meeting itself was all completely inane; buzz words and gobbledygook in every sentence. Nobody could have learnt anything. They were doing this for appearances' sake. The programme was not real, therefore, and couldn't be if it was full of gobbledygook. Buzz words, for example, cannot convey meaning.

What is gobbledygook?

Gobbledygook or buzz words use exaggerated language and are a pretence. Merriam Webster defines gobbledygook as "wordy and generally unintelligible jargon". Buzz words are defined by Wikipedia as "a word or phrase that becomes very popular for a period of time. It may be a technical term and may have little meaning being simply used to impress others." Either way, this is Dilbert territory. Most of his cartoons make fun of business gobbledygook. The problem is that buzz words "become a substitute for a detailed understanding of the business" (Beer and Nohria, 2011, p. 185). Micklethwait and Wooldridge (1996) are arch critics of the language surrounding change and more generally management theory whose "terminology usually confuses rather than educates . . . much of it is incomprehensible gobbledygook" (pp. 12–13).

The quality of communication

Some people focus on the quantity and the quality. "The amount and quality of information that is communicated to employees can influence how employees react [to change] . . . communication is a key factor and its importance cannot be understated in impacting employees reaction" (Wanberg and Banas, 2000). Other people concentrate on the volume of communication. PwC, one of the large consulting companies, has this to say, "Successful organizations see the strategic value in communication with employees before, during and after an organizational transition. Communication must be a constant throughout the entire transition to the new organization" (PwC April, 2012, p. 1). In spite of this emphasis, in practice change efforts often fall down in the sphere of communication, mainly because of the quality of communication. For example, the PwC communication above has several gobbledygook words.

The dilemma, then, is the importance of communication alongside the predominance of gobbledygook.

Key points in this chapter

- Needing meaning in case study A
- Gobbledygook and buzz words
- Needing quality of communication
- Mindfulness and mindlessness
- Cult-like behaviour
- Groupies
- Missing the beat
- Social accounting
- Common buzz words
- Cultivating messianic energy
- Communication aimed at uncertainty

Mindfulness and mindlessness

One important distinction between those who relate to buzz words and gobbledygook and those who do not is whether people are processing information in terms of its meaning (mindfulness) or in terms of its structure (mindlessness). Ellen Langer of Harvard has done some interesting experiments which demonstrate the difference. One experiment she set up revolved around using a photocopier; the experimenters tried to gain access to the photocopier in an office. Different experimenters would come to the photocopier and ask to use it while somebody else was already using it. They asked, "whether they would let us photocopy something" (Langer, 1989, p. 14). There were different reasons given. Some were intelligent and some were not. There were three types of reasons: "Excuse me, may I use the Xerox machine? . . . Excuse me, may I use the Xerox machine because I want to make some copies? . . . Excuse me, may I use the Xerox machine because I am in a rush?" (Langer, 1989, p. 14).

The first and second reasons have the same 'content'. In other words, the meaning is the same. Structurally, however, they are different. This is because the first does not have a reason. The last two reasons, however, are similar because the structure of the sentence is the same (they both have a reason). However, the content (meaning) is different. The second reason is meaningless even though it has a reason.

> If people comply with the last two requests in equal numbers this implies attention to structure rather than conscious attention to content. This, in fact was what we found. There was more compliance when a reason was given – whether the reason sounded legitimate or silly. People responded mindlessly to the familiar framework rather than mindfully attending to the content.
>
> (Langer, 1989, p. 15)

Cult-like behaviour

Speaking and processing information in a mindless manner has an exact parallel with cult-like behaviour emerging on the change team. The company representatives (or internal managers) on the change team became glazed-eyed and leaden-voiced, speaking as if from a script about the benefits of the change programme and reciting some of the mantras of management speak. The fact that this was occurring was known and obvious. It said there was something going on here that was strange. Such cult-like behaviour in a large-scale project like this is unhealthy for the organization as a whole. How could it be otherwise? It tells you to start looking at how

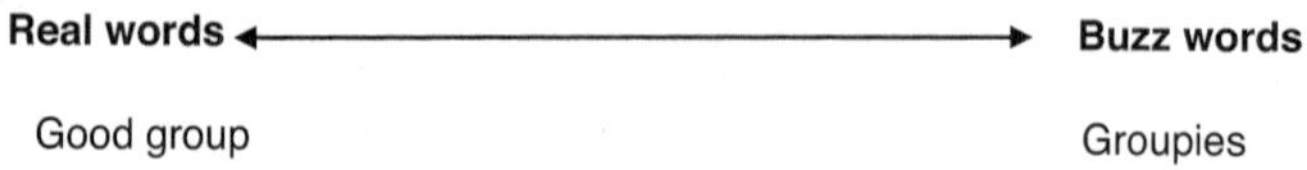

Figure 4.1 The dynamic of real words and buzz words

and why it is happening. It tells you there is something else going on here than simply a programme operating in the best interests of the company and making decisions for good business reasons.

How do you know whether the change is real?

When the change is real, people do not talk in gibberish. Why do people do this? To belong to the group. People obey the 'rules' for that particular group. They don't have a clue how they appear to others, yet their behaviour is based on appealing to others. The latter is why they do it.

Missing the beat

Further on from my time with the financial services company (case study A), I witnessed other effects of speaking exclusively in gobbledygook. Like the financial services company, this organization (case study B) had created an appalling change programme that was managed incompetently. The organization was in the public sector in New Zealand and moderately sized. Because of the sector they were in, there was always pressure on them to change, period, and in particular to cut costs. In the incident I describe in relation to case study B, the focus is on the human resources (HR) branch.

I didn't discover for quite a long time what this change programme was really all about. In fact, unless you were intimately involved in it, you wouldn't have either. I had quite a senior role in this HR branch, but that didn't seem to make any difference. The reason why this situation occurred had a lot to do with woeful communication. In particular, they spoke almost entirely to each other and largely in gobbledygook. They thought what they were doing was wonderful. One of the large consulting companies was hired to lead the change. They also spoke in gobbledygook. They thought, also, that what they were doing was wonderful.

There was supposed to be a stand-up meeting every week run by the branch manager. This was a primary vehicle for communications. Unfortunately, the incumbent was temporary and quite useless. Prior to her, the affable and largely competent branch manager was booted out in a manner that was the cruellest I had come across. The incumbent often cancelled the stand-up for mysterious reasons. We laughed at the time, and winced as well. It was an insult to not have the stand-up. We needed to be communicated with and she treated it like a burden. She did not do her job properly.

When there was a stand-up, a member of the consulting company was often there. In addition, the change leader (responsible for the change in the HR branch) was usually there and spoke. Every word spoken by all of these various people was gobbledygook. Further, all of the people involved on the management/change side did not fully understand the need for two-way communication, rather than 'imparting information'.

Notice that some of the people in HR were too scared to ask anyone anything about the change process. This was simply because they felt like idiots. It appeared that everyone else knew what it was about. But they didn't.

Others' views

I interviewed eight people in two areas of HR, the target of the change programme. These people were either affected by redundancies or close to it. All were intelligent people. Only one could explain the gobbledygook. The rest had just switched off. They had "no idea" what was going on or why it was going on. One said she "didn't get hold of the big story". Another said that they "didn't tell a story about the change". Another said, "I don't know what it was about" (this was the brightest person in our unit). One said,

> I never really knew what it was for, what the real underlying purpose was. I heard all the words but they didn't connect with me . . . I felt removed from it. Never felt part of it. Never had a say. Platitudes were given but we couldn't go and talk [to them]. I asked my team leader but he didn't know the answers either. The further down the food chain you got, you didn't get the whole story. We knew HOW but not WHY. So we couldn't look forward.

This same person added, "communication should have been better. All ways that entail [the communication], going up and down. They were going through the motions . . . [it was] a charade."

My interview with a change leader: case study B

I asked the change leader, who was responsible for the change programme, for an interview and he readily agreed. That in itself told me a lot: he had no sense that I might be critical or even supercritical. Or, if he did know, he didn't care. The latter would fit with the tremendous lack of respect the change team had for anyone not on that team. I was an employee at the time (a rare occurrence as I am mostly a consultant) and on the receiving end of their change programme.

The only problem with the interview was that he spoke entirely in gobbledygook. I could not follow a word he said. It was meaningless buzz words. Half of the time, I couldn't write down my notes and simply zoned out. The interesting thing was that I also interviewed a member of the change team from the organization (an internal staff member) and she likewise spoke solely in gobbledygook. I cut the interview with her short, frustrated and impatient.

In the script that follows Commentary 4.1, the 'operating model' is a template coming from the large consulting company that was hired. It had not been created from scratch for the client, organization B.

Commentary 4.1 The change leader

Change leader for case B	*My questions and interpretation*
	Q: What was the change process about?
A: Aligning the operating model	*What are the key points of the operating model? I need to understand the salience of the operating model. Aligning what with what? This was never explained during the interview. It is* ***without context****.*
	Q: What does transformation actually mean here?
	What are the reasons for the three chunks?
A: It is an HR transformation with three chunks: contact centre, new business partners (new structure) and the HRIS system	*Gobbledygook. What is a 'better HR system'? Why did we need a new operating model: why were no alternative models considered (other than the consulting company's)?*
We have the technology or HRIS system to support the other two pieces. We need to deliver a better HR system. We need a new operating model.	*NB Later in the interview he mentioned that we need to deliver what the business wants and to stop delivering what the business doesn't want. This, however, doesn't really explain anything either. WHAT does the business want? Why isn't this explained in simple English?*
. . . "the broader HR transformation" We need to align with the operating model We needed to design a structure that supports the operating model	*Same as above. I am still in the dark about most of what is said in terms of meaning. All I know is that the focus is totally on 'the operating model'. Why not a focus on 'the strategy' or 'the change process'? IS the 'transformation' the operating model? What IS the 'broader transformation'?*

Commentary 4.2 Interview notes which explain the change leader

Employee's comments	*My interpretation and questions*
	Q: What was the change about?
A: The organization structure for HR has no legitimacy in the organization. Doesn't have the right type of people in terms of capability. Change was therefore about ensuring there was an optimal model the business could buy into. It needed to be customer-focused and have more of an operational focus than a strategic focus. HR had not nailed some of the basic HR response stuff.	*I am beginning to see glimpses of light: there are still lots of 'why' questions (which were never answered anywhere).* *However, it is still a top-down approach, bereft of strategy, and simply a tool of the consulting company to sell some business.*
	Q: Did any (real) change occur?
A: Well there was a large turnover of people. About 50% turnover in HR. That has continued. . . . The new contact centre is working effectively. Nothing else changed except the phone number.	*He's not joking*

The **meaning** in the information outlined above is in the following Commentary 4.2. It is taken from the notes of one of the employees/team leaders. He had also been made redundant. One reason for his comprehension was that he had been for a time on the change team but also he did not rely on gobbledygook.

Gobbledygook doesn't make sense because words exist to impress rather than convey meaning or sense. The priority is to use the same words as those others use. This means the underlying motivation for gobbledygook needs to be tackled: being a groupie.

Case study B demonstrates how bad it can get. Effective communication campaigns tend to reveal rather than conceal and to reduce uncertainty. In this example, the communication generally concealed rather than revealed, and created rather than reduced uncertainty.

Social accounting

The change leader above in the interview notes had not heard of social accounting, nor the responsibility he had to explain himself in a way that was understood.

Social accounting influences the quality of the communication. According to Lines (2005, pp. 157–177), social accounting is defined as the process used for explaining the reasons for the decision to those affected by the decision (cited in Wittig, 2005). To Lines, his findings show that "social accounting . . . [is] positively associated with organizational learning. Further, successful social accounting leads to a positive influence on the likelihood of the [change programme's] implementation success".

One of the projects being worked on in case study B was a new HR information system. Another leader in the whole change effort spoke in exactly the same manner as our previous change leader. She used to explain each week where her project had got to. The basic message was: This was to be "integrated" (jargon) with the "Transformation" (jargon) programme. Almost every word uttered by the manager of this project was jargon. I had no meaning to get hold of so that I could understand the significance of this project. I asked no questions in any meeting. In the meetings with the OD (organization development) team, no one asked any questions about any of it. I knew, later and as explained earlier, that they were none the wiser than me. In which case we were all pretty ignorant. This is the power of using jargon. It silences you. You feel an idiot if you don't know what is being said and even more of an idiot if you repeat the same jargon yourself.

Typical buzz words

- Alignment
- Re-alignment
- Transformation of the company
- Preferred solution
- That's what the business wants
- Preferred partner
- Hitting a milestone
- Deliverables
- Business partners
- On target
- We have a plan
- On plan
- According to plan

Cultivating messianic energy

In one small organization, a client of mine, the branch manager, could not stand one small group. This team was responsible for creating an encyclopaedia. They were 'messianic' to her. I spoke with each of them and found from them and everyone else that they were very high performing. Yet, the criticism that they were 'messianic' stuck and was heard from several people. The danger was that they got people on edge and they were in danger of being axed. Only their high performance stopped them (and they emphasized this repeatedly). My consulting stance was to try to shore them up to safety. They were in a change environment and I had gone there to advise the branch manager.

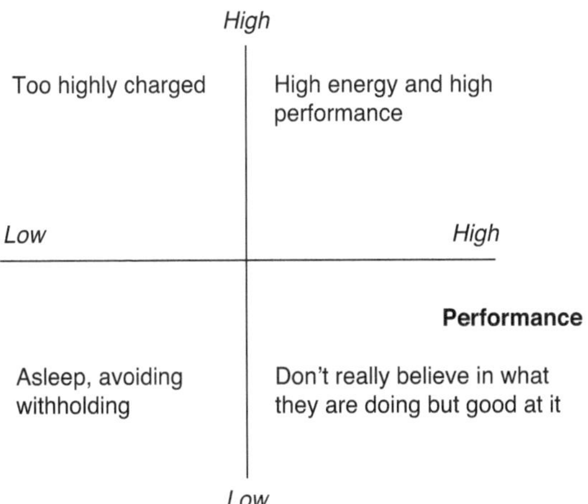

Figure 4.2 Energy and performance

However, my instincts are usually with the messianic groups. I like them. How do you distinguish them from the groupie types who are in love with themselves doing a change effort? The main factor is high performance associated with the positive messianic groups. In contrast, what the branch manager wanted was people who could do their job well but were not high energy or passionate, as this made her uncomfortable. She did not really want people who believed in what they were doing. This distinction is illustrated in Figure 4.2.

Management of uncertainty and emotion

In many organizations, a change programme contains a communications strategy, plan or programme. In this are listed the communication channels to be used at particular times, what information is to be communicated and deadlines for what is sent out. In a change effort, this is insufficient, however common. What is sufficient is based on the necessity to manage emotion compared with just imparting information.

Garvin and Roberto (2011) argue that accomplishing a persuasion campaign calls for a four-part communications strategy.

> Prior to announcing a policy or issuing a set of instructions, leaders need to set a stage of *acceptance*. At the time of delivery, they must

> create a *frame* through which information and messages are *interpreted*. As time passes, they must manage the mood so that employees' *emotional states* support implementation and follow-through. And at critical intervals, they must provide *reinforcement* to ensure that the desired changes take hold without backsliding.
>
> (my italics, p. 18)

Di Fonzo and Brasho (1998) are more specific and emphasize the necessity for "successful programs of change communication [to] hinge upon the proper management of uncertainty associated with change" (p. 295). In other words, communication during change should not be solely for the purpose of imparting information but consciously directed towards a particular emotional state (in Di Fonzo et al.'s case towards the emotional state of uncertainty).

Managing emotion during change

An example of managing emotion during change occurred in a client of mine, for whom I was hired for four years, to interpret for the senior managers what was actually going on in the rest of the organization during the change process. Strictly speaking, this was fulfilling the role of interpreter (described in Garden, 2000, 2015). The overall objective of this change process (the **frame**) was to upskill all the managers in the light of the increased competition in the industry. This objective could have been **interpreted** by the organization as a whole in a negative light, so the senior managers made sure that everyone knew that they included themselves in the upskilling. The difference between this and other clients was the attention paid to finding out from me, who often went walkabout, 'what was going on', that is, **how the managers were feeling**. Most of what we discussed with senior managers concerned the emotional state of the organization. The communication that existed and planned for included informal channels of communication and not just the formal channels. Interventions which were planned by the senior managers could build on (**reinforce**) those areas that were positively intentioned and unpack the meaning of those that were negatively intentioned. In that way, the overall change process was actively managed.

Ten questions about gobbledygook and buzz words

1 Do you understand what gobbledygook is?

....

....

2 If so, give some examples

....

....

3 If not, why not?

....

....

4 Does gobbledygook turn you off?

....

....

5 Are people who speak in gobbledygook, groupies?

....

....

6 What is prompting their groupie behaviour?

....

....

7 Are there pockets of the organization more than others who speak gobbledygook?

....

....

8 Has gobbledygook got worse in your organization in recent years?

....

....

9 What do you do to fend off those who speak gobbledygook?

....

....

10 Do you like gobbledygook? If so, what is the point of it?

....

....

Checklist 4.1 On yourself

This is a checklist of 10 questions for others to answer about **yourself** to gauge gobbledygook. Feel free to copy the checklist and use. Distribute to a minimum of 10 people. The context is the change programme you or your organization as a whole are engaged in.

	1	*2*	*3*	*4*	*5*	*6*	*7*
	Minimal			*Average*			*Brilliant*
1 Am I free of buzz words and gobbledygook?							
2 Do I speak in words that convey meaning, not in gobbledygook?							
3 Can you understand what I am saying?							
4 Am I free of fad projects?							
5 Do I exist in the real world?							
6 Am I free of cult-like behaviour?							
7 Do I understand the difference between meaningful and meaningless communication?							
8 Am I good at two-way communication?							
9 Am I good at social accounting?							
10 Do I take account of uncertainty and other emotional states when communicating?							

Checklist 4.2 On the change team

This is a checklist of 10 questions for others to answer about the **change team** to gauge gobbledygook. Feel free to copy the checklist and use. Distribute to a minimum of 20 people. The context is any change programme they or your organization as a whole are engaged in.

	1	*2*	*3*	*4*	*5*	*6*	*7*
	Minimal			*Average*			*Brilliant*
1 Is the change team free of buzz words and gobbledygook?							
2 Does the change team speak in words that convey meaning?							
3 Can you understand what the change team is saying?							
4 Is the change team free of fad projects?							
5 Does the change team exist in the real world?							
6 Is the change team free of cult-like behaviour?							
7 Does the change team understand the difference between meaningful and meaningless communication?							
8 Is the change team good at two-way communication?							
9 Is the change team good at social accounting?							
10 Does the change team take account of uncertainty and other emotional states when communicating?							

Checklist 4.3 On the senior management team

This is a checklist of 10 questions for others to answer about the **senior management team** to gauge gobbledygook. Feel free to copy the checklist and use. Distribute to a minimum of 20 people. The context is any change programme they or your organization are engaged in.

	1	*2*	*3*	*4*	*5*	*6*	*7*
	Minimal			*Average*			*Brilliant*
1 Is the senior management free of buzz words and gobbledygook?							
2 Does the senior management team speak in words that convey meaning not gobbledygook?							
3 Can you understand what the senior management team is saying?							
4 Is the senior management team free of fad projects?							
5 Does the senior management team exist in the real world?							
6 Is the senior management team free of cult-like behaviour?							
7 Does the senior management team understand the difference between meaningful and meaningless communication?							
8 Is the senior management team good at two-way communication?							
9 Is the senior management team good at social accounting?							
10 Does the senior management team take account of uncertainty and other emotional states when communicating?							

5 Behaviour, not just strategy and structure

The core of the matter

> Our main finding . . . is that the central issue is never strategy, structure, culture or systems. All those elements, and others, are important. But, the core of the matter is always about changing the behaviour of people. And behaviour change happens in highly successful situations mostly by speaking to people's feelings.
>
> (Kotter and Cohen 2002, p. x)

In one client, a large global manufacturing company based in the UK, there was much talk of the difference between being an old economy versus a new economy company. The senior managers talked as if they were new economy (they weren't). One day they presented their annual report at a press conference. I met a group of senior managers the day after. The views in the newspapers were unanimous: this was still an old economy company. The senior managers were furious. I had seen the material presented to the media etc. and blurted out that their material was, in itself, old economy, not new economy. They didn't like this interruption and there was silence for quite a while. My colleague backed me up and we did, for a moment, have a brief conversation about whether it was indeed possible they were old economy. This part of the conversation did not last very long. Their behaviour at that minute was something I would characterize as old economy: rigid, stubborn, not liking the interruption of a young female etc. A new economy response would have been flexible and open. Their behaviour mattered. It told me volumes about how easy or difficult they were going to be to get behaviour change throughout the organization, which they needed in order to create their next-generation solutions (the point of a series of workshops I was designing for them with my colleague).

Unfortunately, I fell ill soon after and had to cancel out of the whole programme. My replacement consisted of two very senior and famous consultants, one from the UK and the other from the US. The former was a strategy consultant. He recommended, very quickly, that they do a re-structure to achieve the behaviour change the company needed. The American focused on mental agility with no emphasis on feelings or emotions. A re-structure was the last thing they needed and simply diverted the whole organization from the real, difficult behaviour change that was desperately needed: creativity and flexibility.

Focusing on behaviour

The desired organizational change or transformation will not happen if you do not focus on behaviour in your analysis, measures and actions (the fifth deadly sin). You are kidding yourself and others if you focus only on strategy, structure or systems. It goes further than this, however. Some organizations think they are addressing behaviour change by virtue only of the strategy or structure change. In other words, through the latter they believe they will automatically create the required change in behaviour. However, as Beer et al. state, one of the two key wrong assumptions managers often make is "that employee behaviour is changed by altering a company's formal structure and systems" (2011, p. 178). The most common consequence of this assumption is that organizations keep restructuring over and over again. They do this because of their mistaken belief that this easy task, of re-drawing the lines of the organization chart, will solve the organization's problems or challenges. It is a deceptively easy task compared with the difficult work of changing behaviour, which most managers are not very good at achieving.

It requires knowledge of and skills in working with behaviour and attitudes, and a psychological foundation. In neither main case study of this book were these requirements met. On the contrary, they were weaknesses. They are usually weaknesses in other organizations as well. Unfortunately, that does not mean they can be ignored. Somehow, attention to behaviour and feelings must be carried out even if the managers and consultants involved are not good at them. Academics have tended to allow for these basic points but that is not matched, in my opinion, by organizations in practice.

Cost savings

I once interviewed for the role as change agent for an organization who insisted that they were not involved in a 'change programme' but a 'transformation'. Their assessment of me was partly based on my using the word 'transformation' and not 'change'. It meant a great deal to them that they

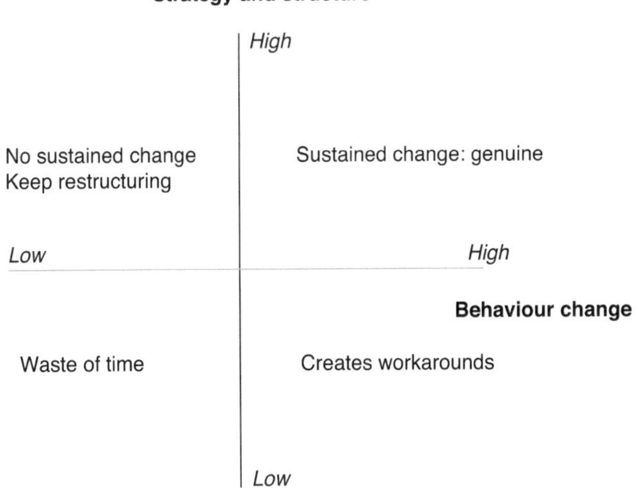

Figure 5.1 Strategy/structure or behaviour change

had this label. What did it matter? Not much. What mattered was whether they focused on behaviour change, not the label they used to describe what they were doing. In a 'people business', the cost of people is, by definition, high. That merely makes it more important to get the people bit right. It is in this kind of business that a cost savings programme is likely to be implemented and involve the shedding of staff (see Chapter 8). A mistake many companies constantly make is to concentrate only on cost savings, and then call what they are doing a 'transformation' or a 'change' programme. It isn't. The results of these choices are portrayed in Figure 5.1.

As Figure 5.1 illustrates, the optimal place for an organization to be is with high levels of change in strategy or structure (or systems) *plus* high levels of change in behaviour. Without the latter, you will not get sustained change but 'keep restructuring'. Without the changes in behaviour or in strategy and structure, everything is a bit of a 'waste of time'. People engage in 'workarounds' when there is a change in behaviour but not a commensurate change in strategy, structure or systems.

Key points in this chapter

- Change won't happen if you ignore behaviour
- A focus on structure alone, in particular, is kidding yourself

- Case study A
- An attitude problem in case study B
- 'No time' for the change process (case study B)
- The consultants are pleased with themselves again
- Pure lying
- Cost savings/redundancies do not make a transformation
- Some good examples of behaviour change
- Engineering system versus a human system
- Living systems
- Basic principle: self-organizing

Case study A

In the finance company, there was a focus on strategy, structure and systems with virtually no focus on behaviour. In the end, the attempt to create a strategy was dropped because of the discord arising from the change programme, and the company was left only with a preoccupation with structure and systems. There was, however, a lot of general talk about the **required** management behaviour with their brave new world but not a focus on how to get that required behaviour. They imagined it would come from hiring new people and from the flow-on effect of the change in systems and structure. The talk about the required management behaviour served to make existing managers feel inadequate, because the new management behaviour was always discussed as a contrast with the calibre of the managers they had already. The new required behaviour was allied to chaos theory which most of the existing managers didn't understand. The idea that, in that sedate company, they would put chaos theory into practice was ridiculous. The notion of chaos theory did not emanate from any real analysis of the company's requirements; it was simply a fad word and idea (Chapter 4). In summary, there was little to admire in the change teams' or the consultants' attempts to improve or create behaviour change.

Case study B was even worse

In this case study, the aim was to restructure, period (see Commentary 5.1). This was formulated by the large consulting company with input from senior managers. The 'behaviour' to arise in the HR personnel who were the target of the restructuring was dealt with indirectly by a few facilitated sessions with the consulting company, who pretty much focused on the restructure. If they had the slightest comprehension that they needed the people present to change their behaviour in response to their structural and systems changes, they didn't show it. I genuinely believe the consultants truly did not know that real behaviour change was necessary to implement the new structure. In addition, there was

Commentary 5.1 The change leader and the employee/team leader

Change leader	*Employee/team leader**
There was an overall requirement to reduce [the number] of full-time equivalents in human resources [HR]. HR transformation [was] in order to deliver what the business wants. . . . The new strategy was designed around this.	The HR strategy was tacked on at the last minute, as an afterthought. It is doomed to failure. *The change leader starts with the stance of reducing the number of full-time equivalents (costs). Then he uses the transformation word.*
The service centre was established in line with the operating model. The intent was to change the way business was interacting . . . change the way business engaged with HR.	There was a desire to help [business] managers understand what these [HR] changes meant to them but they never did [in terms of behaviour]. *Managers had to change their behaviour to make the operating model work but there were no efforts made to make sure that behaviour change happened.* There were good intentions when they started . . . but the [senior manager] involved was ultimately about savings and no business imperative.
We need to deliver better HR service because the business said they didn't want what they were getting.	I understood that in some way we needed to re-align the way we operate with the business. [Basically] it is to cut costs and use less resources. . . . If any change process existed, it was simply to cut costs. *This lack of clarity and precision are all painfully obvious to the employees watching who were left with the conclusion that there was no clear strategy, only a restructure to cut costs. Why not say that then? Also, there is no targeting of the real issue: behaviour and attitudes. There was no real transformation.*

* Author comments are in italics.

an enormous attitude problem to deal with. In the end, the consulting company didn't have time for a change **process** and publicly cancelled it for that reason; they had run out of time. The restructuring, with redundancies, however, went ahead! (They had distinguished between the change programme which they were running and the change process which was concerned with the behaviour).

The problem they needed to address was a much bigger behavioural one – that branch needed to learn to put the needs of the business first. You can't restructure for that particular behaviour change. They needed to concentrate efforts on behaviour, feelings and attitudes etc. But, the employees and managers resented the removal of the previous branch HR manager, who was widely liked. They resented also the introduction of a contact centre which the operational HR people needed to 'man'. They didn't really or fully buy in to the claims that the business didn't approve of what they did as HR. (This was the core of the change programme.) Unfortunately, it was the way the consultants and change team went about their change programme that led to the attitude problem.

During all this, the senior managers didn't have a clue. They were led by the nose by the large consulting company, who spent time getting a follow-up consulting contract with them. Mostly, both groups were incompetent with human beings compared with business, technology, things, structure. As a result, actual behaviour became more out of control than otherwise.

Pure lying

In general, lying occurs on change or transformation programmes when the consultants ignore the necessity to deal with the required behaviour changes which are necessary for the change effort to work or be successful.

Pure lying exists when each of the following exists:

1 Self-deception: people who have to implement the change are not on board (Chapter 1)
2 Vanity and arrogance: the change team thinks they are above everyone else (Chapter 2)
3 Destructive not cohesive: there is no 'one' organization or one branch (Chapter 3)
4 Gobbledygook: every buzz word you could ever find is used by the change team and their acolytes (Chapter 4)

In the two case studies, all these were present.

Cost savings, not transformation

In the commentary above, I have set out the words of the change leader describing aspects of the 'transformation', as he calls it. These words are countered by those of a separate interview with an employee/team leader. As we can see:

- There was no real guiding strategy after all
- There was no real attempt at getting the change in behaviour required
- It was a programme publicly stated to be a transformation of HR but was in fact a cost-savings effort

Keys to doing it right

- Take the change **process** seriously (cf. change programme)
- Don't lie about the **importance** of behaviour in the change programme
- The change programme may take **longer** than you want it to
- It may **cost** more than you want it to
- You **still** focus on behaviour in spite of the above

- Make sure you have people around you who understand **behaviour**
- Make sure you have people around who understand **emotional** things
- Make sure you **interpret** behaviour not accept it at face value
- Have an **invisible leader** in the organization i.e., a clear purpose. This is not the CEO or anyone in the consulting company.

Pleased with themselves

None of the consultants in either organization case study (A or B) knew what they were doing. Yet the change teams thought they were doing a marvellous piece of work. They knew how to re-draw an organization on a piece of paper and sell it to senior managers.

Why are consulting companies so pleased with themselves? Because they create artificial, irrelevant measures that are beside the point. They have stretch goals, but these are always achievable. They want to look good to the client, so they reduce the deliverable target when they run into a problem (Chapter 6).

Why does collusion with the consulting company occur? Being naturally polite; fear for one's job; an opportunity to preen in front of senior managers; learning; the consultants are nice likeable people. What there is less of is confrontation, compromise and negotiation. All the latter are necessary. The large consulting companies are incompetent at the things that matter, i.e., dealing with behaviour, attitude and feelings. They should not be left to run the show.

Things not to do

- Put your head in the sand
- Try and control the control process
- Try and measure everything
- Assume everything in the change process is linear
- Depend too much on the CEO

Successful change processes

Organizations who do it 'right' or 'OK' often have the same sources of incompetence as those who mess up, but they don't lie to themselves about it. Four examples where the organization was transformed but there was minimal re-structuring follow. Each of them majored on behaviour and attitude change as well as attending to the feelings of participants.

Example one

This was a retail company in the UK. A group of external senior managers had bought out the ailing company. They wanted a team of external consultants to engender precise behaviour change in their most senior direct reports. These people were regional managers positioned over the in-house store managers. All of the RMs came to five-day retreats. The managers were not used to management workshops, but the new external senior managers required behavioural change. The key changes were to take more responsibility, resourcefulness and creativity, and the behaviour changes to go with the new strategy and systems. The workshops were behavioural, attitudinal and psychological. How was this achieved?

- We were required to be proactive and constructive around the new strategy
- We were engaged with the behaviour changes required as they occurred on the workshop
- We were able to change the managers' attitudes and for them to lead a change in attitudes by staff (i.e., to be more positive). To do this we had to confront forcefully the buckets of negativity and hopelessness that existed.

Example two

This was a successful insurance company. A network of colleagues, led by myself, spent five years gradually engaging all the managers as well as staff in changing behaviours based on individual need as well as organization need.

How was this achieved?

- The vehicles for doing this were partly a continuous series of workshops (the nature of which altered across time)
- Participation in meetings, interviews, surveys and numerous meetings with the primary senior managers involved in the change process
- Reactions by middle managers and staff informed the whole debate in the company about where it was going. The pure consulting angle was how behaviour change worked in this company. For example, it was behaviour change which led to changes in strategy, not the other way around.
- The managers and staff participated hugely in the whole process.
- The primary virtue required while engaged with the process was patience. The primary need in behaviour from managers and staff was innovation.
- A ton of psychological knowledge was required to wade through the turbulence arising once the change process had traction

Example three

In this example, a computer services company, they needed more relationship-friendly customer behaviour from their customer engineers.

The senior team invested time and money putting all engineers through a three-day workshop concentrating on people skills.

How was this achieved?

- Having time to convince customer engineers of the need for this
- Commitment from the top
- Behavioural/attitudinal/psychological foundation. The primary behaviour required was experimentation and creating patterns of relationships with customers and each other. The company didn't need engineers reading from a people-based script.
- In addition to the three-day workshop, one of the consultants spent a great deal of time with the hiring manager and other senior managers discussing the changes occurring in the behaviour-based workshops and leading them through consideration of other things required in the company to fulfil the overall aims of the change strategy.

The final example was a manufacturing company in the UK. Two colleagues and I had a series of workshops for the top 200 managers. The workshops focused on implementing a new strategy. The context in the workshops was business focused, but the facilitation was also around behaviour (i.e., agility, letting go control, taking risks). In spite of a relative lack of explicit attention to this behaviour, the required behaviour change in the company occurred in practice. This was partly because the required changes were implicit in the design of the programme. The main thrust of the business-like changes agreed through the workshops was about releasing controls. While they came thudding down, people started to behave with agility with great alacrity and make appropriate business decisions. The behaviour change worked because of the strong culture that existed which allowed rebelliousness and independence. Therefore, there was a tremendous impact through individual behaviour change. No restructuring was carried out.

How was this achieved?

- We allowed a wide range of behaviour (to role model letting go control)
- We took risks with the programme (to role model risk taking)
- We had little prepared material so that we reacted intellectually and emotionally on the spot (to role model agility)

Engineering systems and human systems

When we are engaged with a change programme or change process, we are not dealing with an engineering system but a human system. It is not a system with machines but a system with human beings. Because

Table 5.1 Engineering system and human system

Engineering system	Human system
Assume complete rationality	Assume differences in motivation
Assume pure logic is correct	Assume feelings are allowed
No space for accidents or spontaneity	Spontaneity is welcome
Emotion excluded	Emotion included
Machine-like	People-like
Linear	Non-linear
Sequential	Non-sequential
Flows	Paces
"It stands to reason"	"We are just human beings"

you are working with a human system and not just an engineering one, things will happen that are not expected. Table 5.1 sets out the key aspects of both.

Many consulting companies run their change programmes as engineering systems, not human systems. They may talk of human beings but that isn't what they focus on. An engineering system assumes rationality in people's behaviour, much as in conventional economics. The aim is for purely logical approaches and reasoning. There is an assumption that you should have complete control so accidents don't occur, nor spontaneity. Emotion is feared and so, therefore, not allowed in an engineering system. The mechanics of an engineering system is machine-like and assumes linear movement forward, which is sequential and flows.

Living systems

According to Capra, "From the systems point of view, it is evident that one of the main obstacles to organization today is the – largely unconscious – embrace by business leaders of the mechanistic approach to management" (Capra and Luigi, 2014, p. 315).

Organizations have a dual nature (the business aims and communities of people interacting). This is why organizational change can be so fraught and frustrating. The 'people bit' is profound and, over time, shows itself to be unable to be changed in a simple mechanistic manner.

> Many CEOs are disappointed about their efforts to achieve change, in large part because they see their company as a well-designed tool for achieving specific purposes, and when they attempt to change its design they want predictable quantifiable change in the entire structure. However,

> the designed structure always intersects with the organizations living individuals and communities for whom change cannot be designed.
>
> (Capra and Luigi, 2014, p. 316)

Linearity

One important assumption you make in relation to change, or to living systems, is whether change is linear. Most people in practice make this assumption. However, according to Syantek (1997),

> there is a growing appreciation within science . . . that some systems are characterised by nonlinear behaviour. [His approach] proposes that nonlinear systems concepts provide insights into the description of social system behaviour in general and organization change in particular.
>
> (p. 16)

Amis et al. (2004) completed an interesting empirical study on whether an organization made decisions and actions that were linear or non-linear. They found that decisions and actions during a change process were non-linear. Certainly, the more important ones were. Linear processes occurred with activities that were more bureaucratic and less important. By non-linear, they meant the decision process was interrupted by particular events or activities, some random, and then progressed.

> Elements in an organization undergoing a radical transformation will change in a nonlinear manner . . . linear transitions occurred almost exclusively in areas that were uncontroversial, easy to implement, and relatively insignificant with respect to their impact on the traditional operating methods of the organization . . . change in [other] areas was much more likely to be characterised by delays and reversals.
>
> (p. 33)

Self-organization

An interesting and useful concept from a life sciences model is self-organization. This is described by Kauffman (1995), as "the root source of order" (1995, p. vii). "the emerging sciences of complexity begin to suggest that . . . order is not all accidental, that vast veins of spontaneous order lie at hand (p. 8)." This self-organization applies as much to organizations as to the natural world. Kauffman describes this application to the world of business as follows "No single person at IBM . . . knows the world of IBM, yet collectively, IBM acts" (p. 246).

Distributed intelligence

Pascale, in describing the idea of distributed intelligence, described a group of selected leaders, characterising their gifts as related to distributed intelligence: "None of these men led in a conventional fashion. Each unleashed his organization's distributed intelligence." Most of them "came fully to terms with their organization as living systems" (Pascale et al., 2000, p. 37).

The concept of self-organization is not much in abundance in most change programmes I have seen. It requires a certain faith to let it rip. I saw one client who emerged in abundance – a computer company where the changes initiated by the consulting team were amplified extremely by the organization. This occurred by the culture and practice in the organization, which was full of self-organization assumptions.

My experience with self-organization

I had an experience with self-organization in the organization in case study B. This occurred with the engagement project, for which I had responsibility. Fortunately, I was left pretty much on my own to manage this responsibility. I had selected, with advice, a team of 13 lead champions who met with me every week. There were no hierarchical distinctions; all were at the same level according to me. I managed these in a slightly unstructured way. I would explain what engagement meant, how important it was, and their role in fostering engagement and creating a successful engagement survey (high response rate). Another key thing I tasked them to do was to find two to three other people from their work area to help them because they wouldn't be able to do all that was going to happen themselves. I also tasked the leads with drumming up support for the survey by, for example, attending their GM (general managers) meetings, talking to the senior management team, and so on; just giving them ideas.

Most left the meetings each week pretty fired up. Two were not because they found my style too unstructured. In between meetings, the 13 leads got moving. They invited other enthusiasts to join in, who invited more enthusiasts. It went far beyond the two to three new invites. However, I took it as a good sign and let it rip. It was a grass roots uprising; perfectly containable if I needed to do so. Pretty soon, I had 85 champions doing things. Except I didn't manage them. The leads did. Except they didn't really either. The 85 ran themselves, forming into groups (or nodes). I contacted them all with two emails only. I didn't once tell the 85 (apart from the leads) what to do. They were mightily productive. The groundswell from everyone in the organization (not just the 85) was great; engagement became a live topic and the survey response rate was 88%. To my mind, it was a classic example of self-organization, an innate ordering principle was at work (see Beer and Nohria, 2011, p. 191).

Ten questions about behaviour and not just strategy or structure

1 Do you HAVE to change behaviour in response to changes in strategy and structure?

....

....

2 What good examples have you had of changes in behaviour in organizational change?

....

....

3 How do you get a change in behaviour in your organization?

....

....

4 What excuses are used about not changing behaviour in a change process?

....

....

5 Does your organization keep restructuring? If so, why?

....

....

6 Where is there lying (if any) in your organization about 'transformation'?

....

....

7 Have you ever run a piece of work in a self-organizing way?

....

....

8 Do you have an assumption that change in your organization is linear or non-linear?

....

....

9 Do you have a metaphor for your organization? Is your metaphor machine-like or life-like?

....

....

10 Do you believe in a life-sciences model of change in your organization?

....

....

Checklist 5.1 On yourself

This is a checklist of 10 questions for others to answer about **yourself** to gauge behavioural change. Feel free to copy the checklist and use. Distribute to a minimum of 10 people. The context is any change programme you or your organization as a whole are engaged in.

	1 *Minimal*	*2*	*3*	*4* *Average*	*5*	*6*	*7* *Brilliant*
1 Do change programmes I am involved with actually deal with real behaviour change?							
2 Do I avoid controlling change programmes too much?							
3 Do I try to get transformation or change rather than just cost savings?							
4 Do I create an invisible leader or purpose for the change programme?							
5 Do I avoid repeated re-structuring?							
6 Am I comfortable with the emotions of behaviour change?							
7 Am I comfortable with the dynamic and energy of a change process?							
8 Do I allow for non-linear movement of change?							
9 Have I run projects along self-organizing lines?							
10 In general, do I behave as if the organization is a human system not an engineering system?							

Checklist 5.2 On the change team

This is a checklist of 10 questions for others to answer about the **change team** to gauge behavioural change. Feel free to copy the checklist and use. Distribute to a minimum of 20 people. The context is any change programme you or your organization as a whole are engaged in.

---

1. Do change programmes the change team are involved with actually deal with real behaviour change?
2. Does the change team avoid controlling change programmes too much?
3. Does the change team try to get transformation or change rather than just cost savings?
4. Does the change team create an invisible leader or purpose in the change programme?
5. Does the change team avoid repeated re-structuring?
6. Is the change team comfortable with the emotions of behaviour change?
7. Is the change team comfortable with the dynamic and energy of a change process?
8. Does the change team allow for non-linear movement of change?
9. Has the change team run projects along self-organizing lines?
10. Does the change team behave as if the organization is a human system not an engineering system?

Checklist 5.3 On the senior management team

This is a checklist of 10 questions for others to answer about the **senior management team** to gauge behavioural change. Feel free to copy the checklist and use. Distribute to a minimum of 20 people. The context is any change programme they or your organization are engaged in.

	1 *Minimal*	*2*	*3*	*4* *Average*	*5*	*6*	*7* *Brilliant*
1 Does the senior management team actually deal with real behaviour change?							
2 Does the senior management team avoid controlling change programmes too much?							
3 Does the senior management team try to get transformation or change rather than just cost savings?							
4 Does the senior management team create an invisible leader or purpose for the change programme?							
5 Does the senior management team avoid repeated re-structuring?							
6 Is the senior management team comfortable with the emotions of behaviour change?							
7 Is the senior management team comfortable with the dynamic and energy of a change process?							
8 Has the senior management team allowed for the non-linear movement of change?							
9 Has the senior management team run projects along self-organizing lines?							
10 In general, does the senior management team behave as if the organization is a human system or an engineering system?							

6 Is the organization better, indifferent or worse?

Re-arranging the deck chairs on the Titanic

In this chapter, we are interested in whether, during an organization change, we have just re-arranged the deck chairs on the Titanic. Things may be new and different but still not *better* (the sixth deadly sin). In other words, 'change' as a programme or effort is not always better for the organization. This contradicts the notion that every change programme is, by definition, 'better'. How do you *know* if the organization is better, the same or worse? Many people don't know.

Most senior managers start change programmes with the best of intentions. I have never come across a sizable group who were overly cynical or manipulative about the change process. I have regarded them as naïve, being so reliant on the good of a change programme, but nevertheless they were positive and honourable in their intentions. Furthermore, most have been above board in hiring a large consulting company. Usually they want the consulting company in order to 'do the job properly'. In case study A, I baulked at the consulting company they chose at the beginning and was subsequently proved to be accurate in my assessment. In case study B, it was dire. I was sitting in a meeting with my organization development team when our boss announced that one of the large (named) consulting companies was to come into the organization and do a transformation programme. A colleague and I had a fit, both yelping immediately. At the sound of the name of the consulting company, we knew there would be large-scale redundancies no matter what the programme was called or what was required. This was our first close encounter with the consulting company, but their name was a code word.

However, the senior managers were apparently okay with this large consulting company because they wanted their crisp, no-nonsense style, and the senior managers wanted redundancies (cost savings) anyway.

Neither organization (case A and case B) had thought through that the change might make the organization worse, or indifferent. They simply automatically assumed that 'change' would be 'better'.

Caring whether the organization is left better, indifferent or worse

In this chapter, we will explore our two case studies to see if their change programme left the organization better, indifferent or worse. The consultants don't really care whether their client is better, indifferent or worse. They care whether they get another contract with either the existing client or a new organization. It is the internal managers who have to care about whether the programme has left the organization better, indifferent or worse.

Key points in this chapter

- Change is not automatically 'better'
- Damage to the finance company in case A
- A big attitude problem in the public sector organization (case B)
- Their measures are fake; nothing but diary management
- The consultants are still pleased with themselves
- Input versus outcome measures
- Inclusion not exclusion
- Assessing your position with three directions
- Assumptions about the nature of change

Damage to the finance company: case study A

By the end of the change programme, the finance company was damaged in several ways, even though progress had been made towards installing a new computer and information system. No strategy had been determined, as this part of the project had been banned along the way. Many activities had been withdrawn because of the existence of the project, or because the project team were deciding something related to one area of the business and no decision could be taken on that area until they had made their report. Most long-term decisions had been put on hold, and work suffered generally because people were in a rather shell-shocked state most of the time.

The effects took a while to become apparent externally, but the company's reputation eventually began to suffer. They began to be seen as 'just another company', as they had failed to retain that clear spirit of uniqueness that had made them stand out in their own way. Their sales were worse even though the market had improved, and I knew of one third-party seller of their products who was refusing to recommend them as a company to potential customers. In other words, their actual performance had been affected by the kinds of events I have described, because the project team's actions and decisions had been fundamentally wrong for this particular company and insensitively implemented. Yet the change team was quite comfortable with what they were doing up until the moment when the board put two and two together and fired the consultants.

Learning from the finance company

There are many lessons we could take from this company. But the important point to me is that none of it needed to occur if the emphasis had been on behaviour and not just on technology and restructuring (Chapter 5), and if they had monitored and measured themselves and their efforts honestly. This was a company that had been successful and which functioned reasonably well, both in terms of business and morale. If we looked at these events from a strategic point of view, we might say that the problem was that there was no defined strategy to put everything into context and guide the right decisions. We could say that there was a problem of culture change that was managed incompetently. Both these assessments would be correct. But they would be beside the point.

Not having a clear strategy was a result of the events that occurred rather than the cause, and even if the company had had such a strategy, it would hardly have altered the kinds of events and effects I have described. The issue of culture change also ignores the full reality of what happened. This is an example where the focus was on reports and deadlines, on what was going on in appearance rather than on the full reality.

Excuses in the finance company

How can the change team not know what a mess they made? What excuses might they make to justify the fact that everything seems to be worse?

- It was the organization's fault
- There were inadequate managers
- The systems were wrong
- The programme was not going fast enough
- They weren't able to fire people (yet)
- They couldn't influence the top guy
- The organization wasn't 'ready' for them

How do we assess case study B, then?

Case study B

Isn't this change programme a success because they have a new contact centre with a new phone number? So what? Was this a 'change'? Yes, it was part of the change plan and they achieved it. But it was nowhere near the 'HR transformation' required and talked about. Is the contact centre a better alternative overall taking into account all the changes required for an HR transformation to occur? Basically, it was an element in a generic template provided by the consulting company which the senior managers 'bought'. What it did to the organization was unclear.

I was on the receiving end of the consulting company's drive to meet their milestones/deliverables. They represented diary management rather than outcome control. Their demands from them were to get information by a certain time, prepare pieces of information by a certain time, attend meetings at a certain time etc. However, these diary management milestones are input measures. They are the one of the reasons the consultants were incompetent at achieving the real objectives. These milestones ignored the extreme reaction of the HR people against the moves planned. The variables that should have been measured were not measured. I don't think they had output or outcome measures. The palpable stance of the consultants to the HR people was 'do it or leave'. Their measure of success would have been 'ran a few facilitated sessions' (input measure) compared with 'changed the attitude of most of the HR group who attended' (outcome measure). An outcome measure specifies what is the difference between 'now' and 'then'. It involves a comparison between where you want to get to and the current state of the organization.

Table 6.1 sets out some examples of the two, input and outcome measures.

Table 6.1 Input and outcome measures

Input measure	*Output measure*
• 'Do it or leave'	• Better attitude of HR to changes
• Diary management: do 'x' by 'y' time	• HR people start initiating activities that overall fit with the changes
• Get the contact centre up and running by a set deadline	• HR people ask to work on the contact centre
• Get their one phone line ready by set deadline	• Staff know how to use the HR phone line ahead of deadline rather than dragging their feet

Outcome measures and including others

Two practices are key to making the change process better, not indifferent or worse. This is the use of outcome rather than input measures, which we have just explored. In particular, the consulting company did not use behaviour as an outcome measure. The second is to include, not exclude, others. Both case study A and B used primarily input measures or diary management and both excluded others.

The issue is whether there is a barrier up between insiders and outsiders. There needs to be more rotation of the troops, including of senior managers. Usually, including others is not done as a best practice. This may be because of the secrecy involved in making certain people redundant. While this is an important factor to consider, the demand to exclude others is overdone. By having a stream of internal people on the change team, you limit the eight deadly sins that prevent effective change. You limit the extent to which the change team kids itself; you stop the arrogance of the internal members on the change team who are no longer exclusive; you have a chance of maintaining cohesion (because there is more widespread input of ideas); you might lessen the amount of gobbledygook; you can more easily focus attention on behaviour; you deal with some of the resistance and forewarn some of the change team about how to limit the trauma of redundancy. Figure 6.1 illustrates.

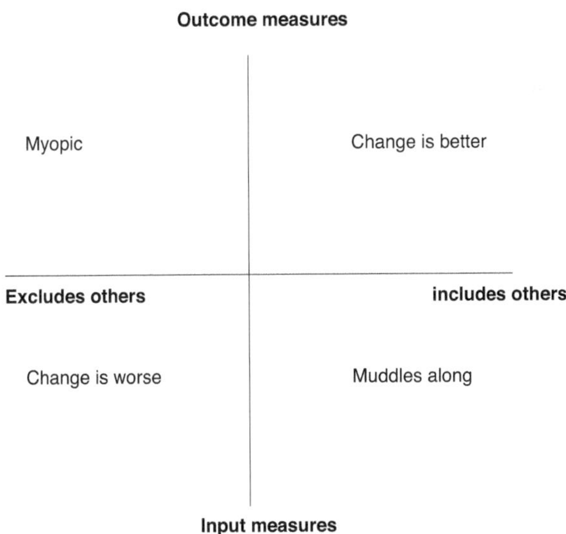

Figure 6.1 Outcome measures and including others

Mapping where you want to get to

The consulting team in case study A tried to have formal measures and a formal procedure to assess the informal or soft aspects of the team. The measure and procedure didn't work. All it did was make sure everyone was *up* by being pleased with themselves for having a procedure like this.

Getting to where you want to isn't going to happen through wishful thinking. Nor will it occur by focusing on milestones that reflect achieving tasks by a particular deadline, which was the mechanism for measuring progress in case study B. In other words, you will not get where you want with input measures.

One of my favourite clients was a senior manager in a global manufacturing/services company. He was always one of the first to adopt our ideas as (networked) consultants. One day when we were chatting with three of their senior managers and two of my colleagues, the senior manager started sounding forth about their frustration with the efforts they made to change their division (there were three divisions in the company, his being the largest). They always had detailed plans and a precise change agenda. They were always committed to the change objectives and were always in line with the organization's change agenda. However, one of the things that happened each year was that they were put under pressure each quarter to meet budget. This meant focusing on selling a few high-priced items. However, the change agenda was that they shift from the large items to higher-margin smaller items. Because of this pressure, they said, the change agenda was never met, even though they earnestly wanted to meet it.

Afterwards I sat down and 'drew' my conversation with the senior manager. It turned out like Figure 6.2.

Interpreting Figure 6.2 is as follows: Note that the lines are jagged not straight. This represents non-linear movement rather than linear movement in the change process (see Chapter 5). Point 0 is the starting point, current time. A, B and C are located one year from now. However, they represent three very different destinations or goals.

A defines the goal where real change is achieved; there is real transformation in the organization. This process includes behaviour. You need action steps and milestones that will take you to A. Achieving this is the quintessential issue of organization change.

B defines change that occurs on pieces of paper but not in reality. This change process doesn't include behaviour. It is indifferent between being better or worse. B means running hard on the change agenda but doesn't really change the organization. B occurs when the change process hasn't really worked and the organization would get to B without a change agenda.

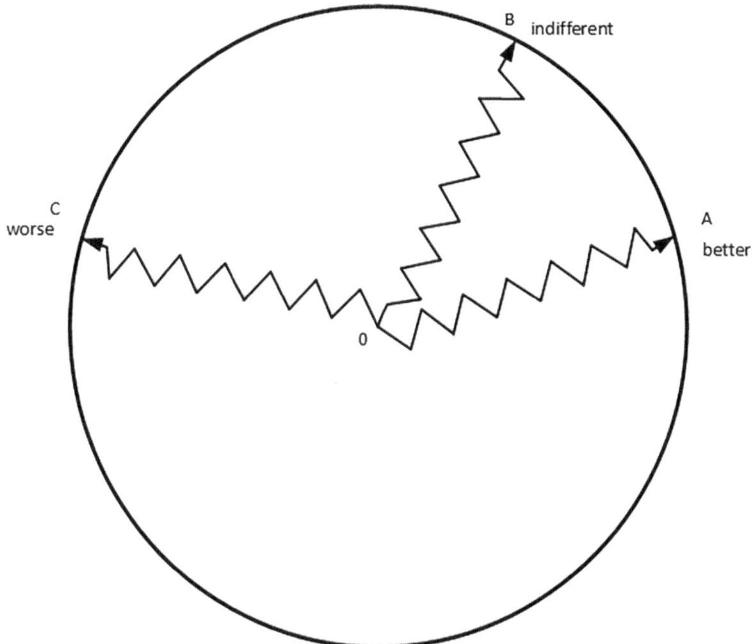

Figure 6.2 Mapping whether the change is better, indifferent or worse

C defines the change programme that leaves the organization worse than before. This is the case study A position. The change programme has gone backwards for the organization. Morale and feelings are worse and little change has been achieved because of internal dissension. Case study B is somewhere between B and C. They are left with an attitude problem in HR and have not really done much but change on paper (position B). Certainly, they have not made the transition they have talked about (position A).

How do you know where you are: A, B or C?

The method is to work out what will be happening if you are going in the direction of A, B and C (see the following). You should map out what each of A, B and C will look like and monitor that you are genuinely heading for A, not B or C.

You think you are at A: **Better**

- You should have evoked a skunk works somewhere along the line
- Morale is up or steady
- People have genuinely changed (for example, they are taking more initiative, taking more responsibility and so on)
- You have monitored culture and the organization's identity
- You have outcome measures, not input measures
- You wrote change objectives to culture and behaviour
- There is an atmosphere of change
- People have moved on from this by now and are now onto something new

You think you are at B: **Indifferent**

- You have been using input measures, not outcome measures
- Your milestones focus on 'finish x report by y time'
- And also on 'gather x information by y time'
- You are walking two paths: one is to 'keep going' straight as before and the other is the path that says 'don't keep going the old way: change'. B never leaves the 'keep going path' because all the measures and pressures from the organization as a whole are to stay on the 'keep going' path.
- You had to ignore change objectives because you had to meet budget
- There has been no behaviour focus
- Everything is essentially the same as before (bewildering)
- You have forgotten your change objectives
- Morale and cohesion are worse
- Frustration
- You know you want to re-structure again
- You are neither better nor worse

You think you are at C: **Worse**

- There is a Holy War somewhere in the organization
- People don't smile
- The consultants focus on their next report to, and meeting with, the CEO
- People don't ask questions at communications events
- Behaviour change isn't there (you don't know what it is supposed to be)
- You haven't calibrated the change needed to get to the right destination
- Input measures, not outcome measures, are used
- You assume change is linear and 100% planned
- The consultants are preoccupied with getting another contract
- You are stymied by some of the same signs as B above

What is the nature of change?

In addition to larger issues around whether the organization is better, indifferent or worse because of the change effort, you need to focus on the nature of change itself, not the nature of the change effort. It is helpful to take a view on what your assumptions about change actually are. If they don't make sense in the cold light of day, change them. Differences in these assumptions between you and your colleagues may be the reason why your change efforts are hitting the rocks.

Organizations change all the time, each and every day if you are an evolutionist. To a revolutionist, this will not be true. Change will only occur at certain 'revolutionary' times.

Ideas on how organizational systems develop and change is shaped at every level of analysis by traditional assumptions about how change works and about what change is. Academic theorists have debated (or dialogued) for years about the nature of change because their assumptions about change dictated their differences. The same is true for practitioners. Some believe in, and apply, a Big Bang approach and others believe in, and apply, a small steps approach. The former is the revolutionary approach and the latter the evolutionary one. What you do in the change effort will vary extremely depending on what you think the nature of change is.

The following section is a diversion into some theorists' ideas about what change is and when it occurs.

Kurt Lewin

One of the first theorists to create a model of organization change was Kurt Lewin (1947). His three-step model has served us well and led the way to many other sophisticated models. It is essentially a Big Bang approach, where change occurs in revolutionary episodes. His model is still widely used today although, because it was originally derived from physics not with human beings, some people have moved to models with a different origin.

Lewin posited three steps to change: Unfreeze, Change or Move, Refreeze. First, we must unfreeze the organization or system in several ways. Only in an unfrozen state will the organization be open to the change needed.

Step two is to change the organization. Now the organization is unfrozen, we are faced with the need to do business differently, create different goals, make the changes that the organization needs.

Step three is to refreeze the organization once the change has been initiated or completed. Systems and processes that reflect the new desired state have to be put in place to make sure the change remains in the organization. Reinforcing the change is needed.

Weick and Quinn

The following sets out how Weick and Quinn (1999) get to a formula of Refreeze, Rebalance and Unfreeze, almost the opposite of Lewin's. Their approach is essentially a small steps approach.

Their analyses of organizational change highlighted an important contrast in change research.

> From a distance . . . when observers examine the flow of events that constitute organizing, they see what looks like repetitive action, routine and inertia dotted with occasional episodes of revolutionary change. But a view from closer in . . . suggests ongoing adaptation and adjustment. Although adjustments may be small, they also tend to be frequent and continuous across units, which means they are capable of altering structure and strategy.
>
> (p. 362)

The phrase 'episodic change' refers to those organization "changes that tend to be infrequent, discontinuous and intentional" (p. 365). This form of change tends to occur in distinct periods. In contrast, "continuous change" refers to changes that "tend to be ongoing, evolving and cumulative" (p. 375). The term used frequently is that change is 'emergent'. This type of change, emergent, over time, produces perceptible and striking organizational changes. The actual change is the same in both instances – the difference in view is wholly perceptual.

According to Weick and Quinn (1999), Lewin's change model assumes inertia, linearity, and so on.

> However, when change is continuous, the problem is not one of unfreezing. The problem is one of redirecting what is already under way. A different mind-set is necessary. But in the face of continuous change, a more plausible change sequence would be freeze, rebalance, unfreeze. To freeze continuous change is to make a sequence visible and to show patterns in what is happening . . . To rebalance is to reinterpret, relabel, and resequence the patterns so that they unfold with fewer blockages. To rebalance is to reframe issues as opportunities . . . reinterpret history . . . Finally, to unfreeze after rebalancing is to resume improvisation, translation, and learning.
>
> (p. 379)

Whichever set of assumptions makes more sense to you, it is helpful to check out those assumptions with others. Differences will lead to disagreement over the path the change effort takes. Similarly, the change team needs to surface their own assumptions about change and check them with people outside the change effort.

Ten questions about being better, indifferent or worse as an organization

1. Are the consultants you hire usually pleased with themselves?
2. Do you focus on input measures and not outcome measures?
3. Can you describe the key features of any soft measures you use?
4. Does the organization usually include others (not exclude them) in each change programme?
5. Do you know if the organization is better, indifferent or worse off as a result of each change programme?
6. Have you ever been ‘better’ in response to a change programme? What did you do to create that?
7. Have you ever been ‘indifferent’ as a response to a change programme? What did you do to create that?
8. Have you ever been ‘worse’ in response to a change programme? What did you do to create that?
9. Do you have a revolutionary or evolutionary attitude to change in the organization?
10. What are the assumptions in the organization about the nature of change? Are they realistic?

Checklist 6.1 On yourself

This is a checklist of 10 questions for others to answer about **yourself** to gauge your understanding of whether the organization is better, indifferent or worse. Feel free to copy the checklist and use. Distribute to a minimum of 10 people. The context is any change programme you or your organization are engaged in.

	1	*2*	*3*	*4*	*5*	*6*	*7*
	Minimal			*Average*			*Brilliant*
1 Do I have a reputation of being good at change management?							
2 Do I challenge consultants on their milestones and whether they are appropriate?							
3 Do I challenge consultants on their measurement of behaviour and attitudes on the change programme?							
4 Do I include others on the change programme more than I exclude them?							
5 Do I focus on outcome measures, not input measures?							
6 Do I think change is automatically 'better' rather than that it might sometimes make the organization worse?							
7 Do I know how to deal with an attitude problem around the change process?							
8 Do I make the difficult trade-offs necessary to make the change programme better?							
9 Do I have clear assumptions about the nature of change?							
10 Have I communicated clearly my assumptions about the nature of change?							

Checklist 6.2 On the change team

This is a checklist of 10 questions for others to answer about the **change team** to gauge their understanding of whether the organization is better indifferent or worse. Feel free to copy the checklist and use. Distribute to a minimum of 20 people. The context is any change programme they or your organization are engaged in.

	1	*2*	*3*	*4*	*5*	*6*	*7*
	Minimal			*Average*			*Brilliant*
1 Does the change team have a reputation of being good with change management?							
2 Do the internal members of the change team challenge consultants on their milestones and whether they are appropriate?							
3 Do the internal members of the change team challenge consultants on their measurement of behaviour and attitudes of the change programme?							
4 Does the change team include others on the change programme more than exclude them?							
5 Does the change team focus on outcome measures, not input measures?							
6 Does the change team think change is automatically 'better' rather than that it might make the organization worse?							
7 Does the change team know how to deal with an attitude problem around the change process?							
8 Does the change team make the difficult trade-offs necessary to make the change programme better?							
9 Does the change team have clear assumptions about the nature of change?							
10 Has the change team communicated clearly their assumptions about the nature of change?							

Checklist 6.3 On the senior management team

This is a checklist of 10 questions for others to answer about the **senior management team** to gauge their understanding of whether the organization is better, indifferent or worse. Feel free to copy the checklist and use. Distribute to a minimum of 20 people. The context is any change programme they or your organization are engaged in.

	1	*2*	*3*	*4*	*5*	*6*	*7*
	Minimal			*Average*			*Brilliant*
1 Does the senior management team have a reputation for being good with change management?							
2 Does the senior management team challenge consultants on their milestones and whether they are appropriate?							
3 Does the senior management team challenge consultants on their measurement of behaviour and attitudes of the change programme?							
4 Does the senior management team include others on the change programme more than exclude them?							
5 Does the senior management team focus on outcome measures, not input measures?							
6 Does the senior management team think change is automatically 'better' rather than that it might sometimes make the organization worse?							
7 Does the senior management team know how to deal with an attitude problem around the change process?							
8 Does the senior management team make the difficult trade-offs necessary to make the change programme better?							

	1	*2*	*3*	*4*	*5*	*6*	*7*
	Minimal			*Average*			*Brilliant*
9 Does the senior management team have clear assumptions about the nature of change?							
10 Has the senior management team communicated clearly their assumptions about the nature of change?							

Part III

Resistance and reactions

7 Resistance from intelligent people

What is resistance to change?

> One of the most widely used mental models that drives organizational behaviour is the idea that there is resistance to change and that managers must overcome it. This idea interferes with successful change implementation.
>
> (Dent and Goldberg, 1999, p. 25)

In my first change assignment in my career as a consultant, I was asked by a team of three senior managers to introduce changes to a successful, interesting company. My first few interventions were with the senior managers. The managing director was the only one who was truly defensive, but he was also relatively easy to get on board. The real work started when I worked with the middle managers. Here we noticed quite a bit of 'resistance'. However, the change team, including myself, did not interpret this negatively. On the contrary, as we went along through the years I was there, we interpreted any resistance as meaning we had done something wrong and we corrected for it. It was this process that told us how to manage and create change in the organization. The middle managers, in particular, were a source of feedback for the organization as a whole. They did slow the whole process down, but it is a moot point whether that was a disadvantage or an advantage. My own opinion was that it meant we could embed the changes more effectively.

Many managers and consultants still have a very simplistic view of what resistance to change is. It "is never portrayed as the product of rationally coherent strategies and objectives" (Ford et al., 2008, p. 363) on behalf of resistors. As a result, we have a distorted view of resistance (the seventh deadly sin). In the general view,

- Resistance is something that must be 'overcome'
- Resistance is something that is bad or wrong
- The change agents are the good guys and the resistors are the bad guys
- The change agents have no resistance to change themselves

In this chapter, we explore these ideas and see how valid they are. Instead of countering each point above, my approach is to end up with a different view of resistance which largely turns these ideas on their head.

Key points in this chapter

- An overview of resistance to change
- Forms of resistance in case study B, the public sector organization
- Forms of resistance in case study A, the finance company
- The meaning of resistance to change
- Losing something of value
- Active and passive
- The consultants' view of resistance
- A different version of resistance – intelligent dissenting adults
- "Resistors don't care about the organization"
- "The consultants know everything about change"
- Other views
- Other explanations of resistance
- Attractors
- Deep structure

Forms of resistance in case study B

When I was an employee for four years, in the public sector, my team resisted the consulting company's change programme in classical and non-classical ways. We laughed at the change team, for example, and their arrogance. Our main resistance, however, was highly destructive. It was to remain quiet, to be passive, to be pained, to be upset, to not be forthcoming. These behaviours were true for those who were made redundant as well as those who would remain employees. We didn't want to cooperate in any way with a management we despised and a consulting company we despised.

Forms of my resistance to change in case study B

- Passivity
- Meekness
- Zero positive intention
- Negativity
- Arguing to myself
- Rebellion
- Subtleties
- Outspoken in certain places

- Avoidance of change team
- Staying out longer for lunch
- Went for numerous coffee catch-ups
- Not working proper hours
- Sitting at desk for months doodling
- Throwing away papers
- Not cooperating with the handover team
- The longer it went on, the worse I became

Resistance to change in these ways takes very little effort. On the contrary, I conducted these with considerable glee. I am normally a highly cooperative and hard-working person. To have carried on like that in this organization was seemingly impossible in the extreme. Why? I was too insulted by the change team. It must have taken some effort for the change team to insult me to that degree. But they did.

So what happened in case study A?

Case study A

In the finance company, I had lots of room to move, so my resistance to the change was far more active. I was an external consultant but I still resisted the change programme furiously. One reason was identical to my reasons in case study B. I despised the consultants and their incompetence at running this particular change programme. Here is what I did:

- Discussed how stupid the programme was with all manner of employees
- Didn't cooperate with the change team ever
- Told the managing director my negative views of the whole programme
- Was on the receiving end of countless phone calls from various employees
- Empathizing with the above
- Having lunch with people who had been fired
- Trying to shore up as many people as possible in the sales division
- And so on

The salient point of these two descriptions is that the change effort should have been so mismanaged that they got such behaviour out of a well-intentioned change-loving person. I am always (to a fault) in favour of change, so even labelling my behaviour as 'resistance to change' is problematic. This dynamic is a common pattern with behaviours called 'resistance'. In case study B, the eight people I interviewed were each change enthusiasts. So, what were they all doing resisting this change too? One reason was that there was no overlap between our collective view and the change agents' view about what was going on. The views were poles apart. But that does not mean the change agent's view was 'correct' and the employees/managers were 'wrong'?

The meaning of resistance to change

Kurt Lewin introduced the term 'resistance to change' as a systems concept affecting managers and employees equally. Lewin (1947), a famous management theorist, derived the idea of resistance to change from physics experiments; specifically, when one object hit another object. The reaction of the one object hitting against the other was termed resistance. However, Lewin interpreted his observations in a particular context, systems thinking, yet that context was largely missing from subsequent users of his idea. It is from these beginnings that the common notion of resistance being a kind of counteroffensive on the part of individuals arose.

However, Lewin evolved his concept "based on the person as a complex energy field in which all behaviour could be conceived of as a change is some state of a field" (Marrow, 1969, p. 30, quoted in Dent and Goldberg,1999, p. 29). For Lewin, resistance to change could occur, but that "resistance could be anywhere in the system". In other words, it could occur in the managers or change agents. For about 30 years after, Lewin's understanding of the term was not strictly carried through, "but was narrowed to a psychological concept affecting employees only" (p. 39).

Losing something of value

One alternative view of resistance to change is that it means the so-called resistor is losing something of value.

> We assert . . . that the best way to challenge the conventional wisdom [concerning resistance to change] is to suggest that people do not resist change per se. People may resist loss of status, loss of pay, or loss of comfort, but these are not the same as resisting change.
>
> (Dent and Goldberg, 1999, p. 26)

Burke's description similarly defines resistance to change as

> not necessarily that of resisting the change per se but is more accurately a resistance to losing something of value to the person – loss of the

known and tried in the face of being asked, if not forced, to move into the unknown and untried.

(Burke, 2014, p. 109)

Other meanings of resistance to change: active and passive resistance

My own understanding of resistance comes from working as an independent consultant for approximately 20 years, including being associated for four years with London Business School, and then being on the receiving end of others' change programmes for four years. It is important to see the resistance as being either active or passive. In my illustration of my own resistance, I included my passive forms of resistance, which can be just as deadly as the active variant. Further, resistance to change can be negative as well as positive. It is not solely negative. It can be positively intentioned to the organization (see later in this chapter). Figure 7.1 illustrates the various forms of active and passive resistance, which can have a negative or positive expression.

An example of positive active resistance is when people take responsibility for describing an alternative to a particular part of the change effort. Passive positive response is when a resistor stays calm but has constructed a

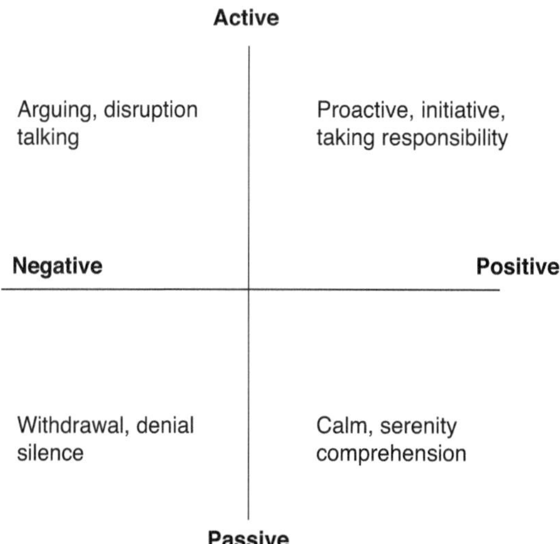

Figure 7.1 Active and passive resistance

different understanding of the change process. The active and passive negative expressions are the obvious known forms of resistance, from arguing to withdrawal.

How the change team/consultants view resistance to change

It is more likely the case that, in practice, the consulting company will walk right over any resistance. They don't care. They do this because they have assumed they are superior when they are not (see Chapter 2). **To the consulting company, resistance occurs when you are not doing what you are told and not viewing the change ideas as marvellous.** Figure 7.2 illustrates.

To the change team, resistance to change comes from lack of motivation and lack of obedience, so that the resistors do not do what they are supposed to do.

Because that is the consultants' view of resistance to change, they do very specific things (see Table 7.1).

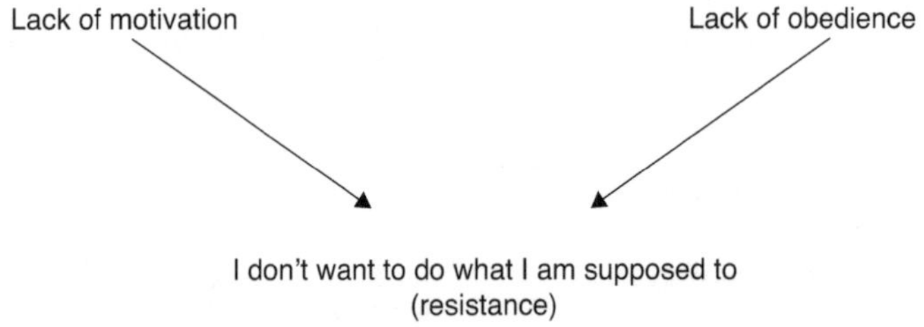

Figure 7.2 Consultants' view of resistance

Table 7.1 The consultants' view of resistance to change

Consultants' view of the problem	*Consultants' response to 'resistance'*
People disagree	Sell the solution
People argue	Argue them down
People are passive	Fire them up, enthuse them
People are flat, no enthusiasm	Only have enthusiasts on change effort
People don't believe in the change	Tell them stories about other organizations
People get bored with the whole thing	Quick wins, move quickly
People don't like change	Keep the whole thing secret
People don't want to do what we want	Order them about

How the change team creates resistance

Because the consulting company has an inappropriate view of resistance and behaviour, they can end up creating resistance. Aside from misinterpreting the resistance to change, and in spite of responding in inappropriate ways to it, the change team can mistakenly and misguidedly *create* resistance. This is illustrated in Figure 7.3. Enthusiasts are those who are treated as intelligent people by the change team. And there is general positivity in the organization. Those who are 'spinning wheels' are trying to change and are willing to change but get flattened by the change team's behaviour. Hence, they get nowhere (spinning wheels). Cynicism arises when they are treated as if they are intelligent by the change team but the general climate in the organization is negative and creates cynicism. Finally, the resistance response is when the people can't get off the ground. They are not treated as intelligent by the change team and the culture/atmosphere in the organization is negative. Resistance is, thus, hard to avoid.

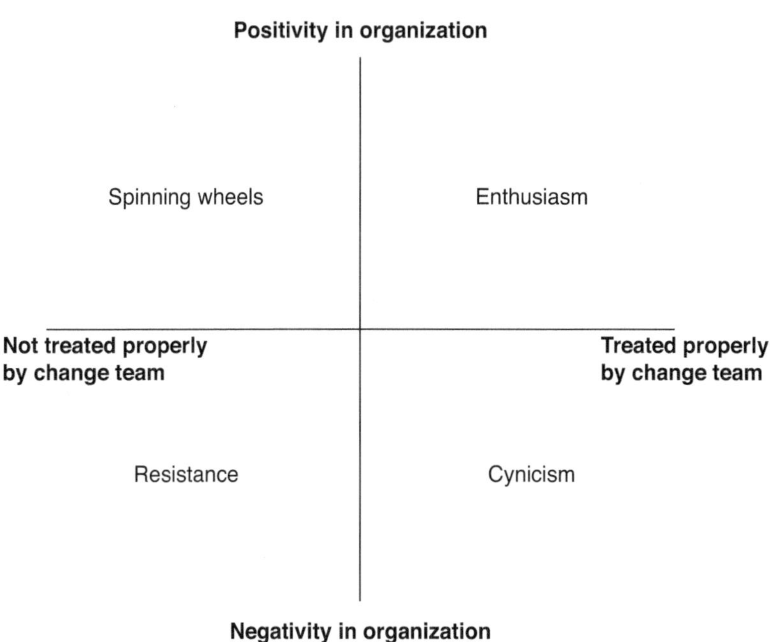

Figure 7.3 How the change team creates resistance

An alternative view of resistance to change

The prevalent existing view of resistance to change is not particularly helpful compared with the reality of what is going on with people's experience of change. In the next few sections, I set out my own formulation. Perhaps the clearest catalyst was my observation that an innocent question was almost always treated as a form of resistance – which is, of course, nonsense.

In both case studies, the resistance behaviours arose because

- People were treated like idiots, not like intelligent adults, especially by the consulting company
- People were also treated as if they didn't care about the organization as much as the change team/consultants
- It is also the case that the change team assumed they know more about change than the rest of us. This was not the case. In case study B, some people knew far more about change processes than the 20–30-year-olds in the consulting team.

In summary, resistance is a reaction to being treated like an idiot who doesn't care about or understand change instead of as an intelligent dissenting adult. Because of this way of being treated, people may not want the change. In any event, they are intelligent dissenting adults.

Intelligent dissenting adults

Resistance means that discussion concerning the change with intelligent people has not occurred. (True consultation did not occur in either case study).

Table 7.2 illustrates.

The most effective mechanism I have ever seen for actively and assertively creating resistance they said they didn't want was in case study B with the 'stand ups' they held. Some of these were branch meetings and others were ad hoc. They were aimed at imparting information. They clearly wanted questions to be asked because they commented on the lack of them regularly. However, they spoke at us as if we were morons. Probably we were more intelligent than they were, but they misinterpreted any signals of

Table 7.2 Intelligent, dissenting adults

Reality	*False Interpretation*
Intelligent	Morons who need explanations
Dissenting; having a different view	Argumentative
Adults	Children who are playing up

interest because they were so stuck in an old-fashioned mental frame about change, change agents and resistors. The forms others' resistance took were similar to my own. Passivity. Blank faces. No enthusiasm. These resistance reactions were only partly to do with the content that they were explaining to us with all their information and slides. It was due mainly to the process, their behaviour and style, the atmosphere they created.

Intellectual IQ as well as emotional intelligence (EQ)

On the organization's side, there needs to be a change effort that creates intellectual change, not just emotional change. We need to take into account participants' IQ, not simply their EQ. Most change efforts focus only on the latter and aim to 'sell' the change, trying to appeal to people's emotions. People have brains as well and their questions and concerns need to be satisfied. We need to spell out the 'reasons' for the change. Quite a few managers I know could not be convinced of the rationale for a merger in case study B, for example. (This merger occurred two years before the change programme in the HR area.) The whole change effort with the merger in practice was focused on the communications/sell job needed to win people over, but little of this was aimed at the underlying intellectual rationale for the merger. Even two years after the merger, people were not convinced of the original rationale.

One excellent manager I knew quite well left; her reason for doing so was the inadequate attention paid to explaining to her and everyone else of the rationale for the original merger. Nor did this individual resist the whole change process in a classical sense. She didn't argue about the change. She wasn't passive. She was the opposite of a 'resistant' person. Her intelligence had been overlooked and offended by the sell job that had occurred.

Mutual power, not dictatorial power

The overall change team in case study B acted, relative to the recipients of the change programme, like Pol Pot. The solution should have been to be mutual (equal in power and status), not dictatorial. For example, when there was lying about the consultation process (in other words, there was no real consultation), the change programme was being dictatorial. If we are dealing with intelligent adults, real consultation should occur.

"Resistors don't care about the organization"

Another common misinterpretation by change agents is that, by being wholly behind the change, they are more concerned about the organization than the remaining employees and managers. If we start with the notion that there is a difference between the change agenda and the organization's agenda, it cannot be the case that the consultants/change agents care more about the organization. The resistance can be, in fact, positively intentioned to the organization. It usually is.

The saddest episode for me in an organization change effort occurred with a long-standing client. Shortly into my assignment, my favourite senior manager was fired/made redundant. He cared more for the organization than any other senior manager there. But he made the mistake of saying he didn't approve of the wholesale change that had begun in the organization. He was promptly fired. It was a stupid response because he could easily have been won over. This is true precisely because he cared so much for the organization. He simply had a different view. Surely the change team can behave like adults and allow for a different view?

Another example was a computer company. Here, the remaining divisions ganged up on the HR division because the latter was seen as always resisting change. My job was to tell them off and get them moving. The frustration of the rest of the organization occurred because they saw the HR group as not caring about the organization but, in fact, they did.

Voices of resistance – the positive intentions towards the change effort

In a psychological mind-set, resistance to change is interpreted as an intelligent positive response. If we assume that the behaviour we're witnessing is positively intentioned, we should look for the intelligence within the message that is sent. Understanding resistance requires that you 'hear voices' or, in other words, hear what is really being said. The latter is hearing the meaning of information rather than the structure of the information. Table 7.3 illustrates some examples of resistant voices you can translate. The second voice is what is *really* being said. All of them are positively intentioned towards the organization, in spite of the fact that there is 'resistance'.

The consultants know everything about change

One of the most common misperceptions prevalent in change situations is that the consultants know everything there is to know about change. In particular, they are thought to know more about change than the internal people do. In our two case studies, that was certainly not the case. What the consultants know is the legal requirements of the change programme, the phases. But, in terms of the change process, they knew far less that the people in the organization they were interacting with. Indeed, I would go so far as to say that skill in the change process – the real dynamic of change – was a weakness in the consultants in both case studies.

Table 7.3 Voices of resistance

What they say	*What they mean*
"They haven't taken me into account"	We have moved too fast
"This won't work here"	We have special conditions
"They don't know what they are doing"	I have expertise that isn't being used
"I don't know who is on the change team"	We need to include people more
"They keep changing things"	We want things to work properly

The resistance and defensiveness of the consulting team

The general stance for those employed in an organizational change effort is that the employees and internal managers (not on the change team) are potential resistors. They are the ones on the receiving end. However, if our objective is a successful change programme for the good of the organization, we need to acknowledge that the external consultants can be resistors in exactly the same manner as employees and internal managers. One of the things we have explored in this chapter is a different perception of resistors and of resistance to change. The exploration does not stop there. We need to perceive change agents/consultants differently as well. Change agents can themselves get in the way of the change effort. They can resist the change process – the true dynamic of change. They do this whilst efficiently managing the technical formal aspects of the legal requirements of change.

One of the main ways that the consultants showed resistance in the two case studies is that they defined their jobs quite narrowly. They defined them in terms of gathering and making sense of information (which they got from all over the organization). This was the first clue that they didn't really know what they were doing. They needed to create change, not collect information. By doing this, they avoided the crunch issues (personal and work) needed to motivate the people in the organization who needed motivating. Senior managers colluded with it all. Which is presumably why the change process is needed in the first place.

What resistance can be seen in the consulting team?

- Don't do real consultation
- Afraid to discuss issues with intelligent people
- Don't encourage real questions
- Can't take challenging questions
- Don't interact widely
- Frightened of emotion
- Won't allow for employees to know more than they do about change
- Haven't a clue about the change process cf. change programme

- Don't understand people
- Name drop
- Boast
- Are arrogant

How to cope with the resistance of the consultants/change team

The same solutions normally posed to the change agents to overcome resistance of employees and internal managers can be asked of the people who have to cope with the change agents' resistance to change. What can you do?

- Ask questions
- Ask them *why* they want the information they are asking you for
- Invite them to coffee
- Talk with them about how you feel about the change effort and the organization
- Make a point of telling them about your qualifications/experience
- Ignore their arrogance
- Tell them why you are doing any of the above

Five golden rules for dealing with resistance to change

The first and foremost principle to use to deal with resistance to change, including not having it occur in the first place, is that the power balance should not be extremely over-weighted in favour of the change agents. The power balance should be equal. This would imply the following five golden rules for dealing with resistance. There should be:

- True consultation (true listening to feedback)
- True participation (true involvement of the greatest number of people)
- Treat people like intelligent dissenting adults
- Explain intellectual rationale as well as EQ rationale
- Don't expect 100% obedience. Don't react when there isn't.

Other views

Other authors in the field have similarly strongly held views. Ford et al. (2008) state

> prevailing views of resistance to change tell a one-sided story that favours change agents by proposing that resistance is an irrational and dysfunctional reaction located "over there" in change recipients. We . . . [propose] that change agents contribute to the occurrence of resistance

> through their own actions and inactions and that resistance can be a resource for change.
>
> (p. 362)

They note, "It is time to expand our understanding of resistance to change, including its sources and its potential contribution to effective change management" (p. 362).

The bulk of studies and management opinion favour the change agent as being blameless and pure while the change recipients, employees and also managers in their turn are wholly unreasonable. Change agents are portrayed as people who deal with the real resistance of change recipients. "There is no consideration given to the possibility that resistance is an interpretation assigned by change agents to the behaviours and communications of change recipients, or that these interpretations are either self-serving or self-fulfilling" (p. 362).

One of their most important points is that most people considering resistance to change do not consider the possibility that change agents "contribute to the occurrence of . . . resistance behaviours and communications through their own actions, and inactions, owing to their own ignorance, incompetence, or mismanagement" (p. 362). Rather, "resistance is portrayed as an unwarranted and detrimental response residing completely 'over there, in them' (change recipients) and arising spontaneously as a reaction to change, independent of the interactions and relationships between the change agents and recipients" (p. 362).

Other explanations of the organization's resistance

Attractors

There are two additional possible explanations of what resistance to change is, its dynamic. Both describe a situation where the organization resists change; people are labelled 'resistors'. The first is part of the understanding of living, non-linear systems (see Chapter 5) and is the concept of 'attractors'. These are complexes of behaviour, attitudes much in the way we think of the core aspects of culture. It is the existence of attractors that arise from patterns of relationships between people that occur during stability that **keeps the organization as it is when attempts are made to change it**. Thinking in these terms (i.e., the patterns of relationships, attractors, non-linearity) create an organization change effort that is more in keeping with others' findings on the nature of change (see Chapter 6). In other words, there are very good reasons to believe that these attractors exist. Attractors are

> patterns of behaviour with the dual characteristics of "sensitivity to initial conditions" and "stability". The former characteristic suggests that

> the early history and founding of an organization is highly significant . . . These initial behaviours are quite specific, if not unique, to the situation [and they are therefore . . .] distinct in nature, are likely to be undetectable at the time, and become entrenched over time as a consequence of consistent reinforcement.
>
> (Burke, 2014, p. 80)

The second characteristic, stability, "can best be understood . . . as an organization's culture" (Burke, 2014, p. 153). Attractors may be responsible, therefore, for the apparent resistance to change that we see in organizations.

Another concept is deep structures

The other explanation for what appears to be resistance to change is the existence of a deep structure in the organization. This approach is explained through the construct of a highly durable underlying order or 'deep structure'. This is what persists and limits change during equilibrium periods and it is what disassembles deep structure, or the organization itself, with wholesale transformation during what is called 'evolutionary punctuations'. Gradualist paradigms (which operate in an opposite manner), in contrast to 'revolutionary' paradigms, insist that systems can 'accept' virtually any change, any time, as long as it is small enough. In these paradigms, big changes result from insensible accumulation of small ones. In contrast, revolutionary paradigms suggest that, for most of an organization's history, there are limits beyond which change can be actively prevented. **These limits can created by the organization's 'deep structure'.** Gersick's definition of this is:

> A network of fundamental, interdependent choices about the basic configuration into which a system's units are organized and the activities that maintain both this configuration and the system's resource exchange with the environment. Deep structure in human systems is largely implicit. . . . [Deep structure] must first be dismantled, leaving the systems temporarily disorganized, in order for any fundamental changes to be accomplished. Revolutions are relatively brief periods when a system's deep structure comes apart . . . Revolutions occur at all because internal changes pull parts and actions out of sync with each other and . . . environmental changes threaten the system's ability to obtain resources.
>
> (Gersick, 1991, pp. 15, 19–20)

Both explanations of resistance to change support the basic stance that 'resistors' are not a negative nuisance. They might simply be acting out the presence of Attractors or a deep structure within the organization.

Ten questions on the resistance of intelligent people

1 Do you believe there is such a thing as resistance to change?

....

....

2 Can you see the point of treating resistance to change as more complicated than a negative event?

....

....

3 Do you think resistance to change relates to the loss of something important to the individual?

....

....

4 Can you see both passive and active forms of resistance to change?

....

....

5 How does your organization deal with the intellectual IQ response to resistance to change?

....

....

6 How does your organization deal with the emotional EQ response to resistance to change?

....

....

7 How do you think the organization should behave to make sure all people are treated like intelligent adults in a change programme?

....

....

8 How does your organization ensure that the relationship with recipients of a change process is mutual, not dictatorial?

....

....

9 Have you encountered change agents/consultants resistant to a true change process?

....

....

10 Can you apply the ideas of 'attractors' and 'deep structure' to any resistance to change in your organization?

....

....

Checklist 7.1 On yourself

This is a checklist of 10 questions for others to answer about **yourself** to gauge resistance to change. Feel free to copy the checklist and use. Distribute to a minimum of 10 people. The context is any change programme you or your organization are engaged in.

	1	*2*	*3*	*4*	*5*	*6*	*7*
	Minimal			*Average*			*Brilliant*
1 Do I deal well with resistance to change?							
2 Do I remain calm when faced with resistance to change?							
3 Do I know how to galvanize people so they are contributing positively to the change effort?							
4 Do I treat people as intelligent adults?							
5 Do I consult sufficiently?							
6 Do I assume that 'resistors' care about the change effort too?							
7 Do I explain the intellectual rationale for change?							
8 Do I explain change in terms that are high in EQ or emotional intelligence?							
9 Do I allow that there will not be 100% obedience?							
10 Do I know how to move on from any change effort?							

Checklist 7.2 On the change team

This is a checklist of 10 questions for others to answer about the **change team** to gauge resistance to change. Feel free to copy the checklist and use. Distribute to a minimum of 20 people. The context is any change programme you or your organization are engaged in.

	1	*2*	*3*	*4*	*5*	*6*	*7*
	Minimal			*Average*			*Brilliant*
1 Does the change team deal well with resistance to change?							
2 Does the change team remain calm when faced with resistance to change?							
3 Does the change team know how to galvanize people so they are contributing to the change effort?							
4 Does the change team treat people like intelligent adults?							
5 Does the change team consult sufficiently?							
6 Does the change team assume that 'resistors' care about the change effort too?							
7 Does the change team explain the intellectual rationale of change?							
8 Does the change team explain the change in terms of EQ or emotional intelligence?							
9 Does the change team allow that there will not be 100% obedience?							
10 Does the change team know how to move on when the change has finished?							

Checklist 7.3 On the senior management team

This is a checklist of 10 questions for others to answer about the **senior management team** to gauge resistance to change. Feel free to copy the checklist and use. Distribute to a minimum of 20 people. The context is any change programme you or your organization are engaged in.

	1	*2*	*3*	*4*	*5*	*6*	*7*
	Minimal			*Average*			*Brilliant*
1 Does the senior management team deal well with resistance to change?							
2 Does the senior management team remain calm when faced with resistance to change?							
3 Does the senior management team know how to galvanize people so they are contributing positively to the change effort?							
4 Does the senior management team treat people as intelligent adults?							
5 Does the senior management team consult sufficiently?							
6 Does the senior management team assume that 'resistors' care about the change effort too?							
7 Does the senior management team explain the intellectual rationale of the change?							
8 Does the senior management team explain change in terms of EQ or emotional intelligence?							
9 Does the senior management team allow that there will not be 100% obedience?							
10 Does the senior management team know how to move on when the change has finished?							

8 The deep trauma of redundancy

Voices of redundancy

Person A in case study B:

> I got a letter saying "you have been made redundant . . . Your role has been made redundant". My concern was: what is the period [for it]? My brain was pragmatic: What do I need to do to get a job? . . . The visibility of management [during this period], in general, was very poor. My boss wasn't checking in with me. . . . This was the most difficult time [of all] that I had had and [at the same time] I got the least support from my boss while working at [the organization]. The harder it got for managers, the more they backed away.

Person B in case study B:

> As an employee the [change process] was not managed well, we needed clarity on things that were happening. Some people need more input than others; reassurance and deeper understanding. Managers need to appreciate that and they didn't do so particularly well. The change process . . . is where good leaders step up and shine and average managers do not. We have a lot of average managers not good at leadership in that context. When in a change context, you need leaders; if not there is churn, conflicts and confusion.

The two people quoted above had been made 'affected' people and subsequently made redundant. The voices are different in their detail but similar emotionally. There is a sense of lack and loss, that the experience is difficult, and that the episode is not handled well. People should be treated as if they were in a people business. They weren't.

The grief and loss associated with work life

This chapter looks at that difficult phenomenon of redundancy. Here we look at the change team in case B, the people made redundant as well as the managers of the latter. While I am critical of the latter, the emotional context of the changes was set by the senior managers and the change team. These people were incompetent but they were also cruel. It is the latter deadly sin that we focus on in this chapter.

We zero in on some interviews from case study B which illustrate the reality of the redundancies. The first point is that redundancy is far more important to each individual than we often allow in this world, where it has become common. Pascale et al. (2000) state

> The role of . . . society, is an essential piece of the puzzle. It sets the context for appropriate levels of reciprocity. Cultural norms suppress or dignify human expectations and organizational ambitions. To date, social awareness does not acknowledge the grief and loss associated with work life as among the most painful of human experiences, ranking alongside divorce and the death of a loved one.
>
> (pp. 266–267)

In what follows, I refer to the interviews of some of the eight people who were made redundant in the HR branch of case study B. I had no idea of any grief or sense of loss in these people until the interviews; until then it was covered up. To others in the organization it would similarly have been covered up. People pretended they were perfectly all right when they weren't. I look also at what I call the 'outsourcing of emotion'; in other words, the outplacement service that was offered us. I was the only one who went to outplacement (to see what happened there). No one else would go. I thought it was seriously useless in reality. However, its existence says a lot about the organization (case study B) who arranged for people to go there because they were so inadequate at dealing with emotion themselves.

Key points in this chapter

- Being left alone by the managers
- Acknowledging grief and loss
- Why the redundancies?
- Psychological as well as legal contract: reciprocal obligations
- Derivation of deep trauma
- Two different case studies
- Dealing with emotional issues

- Need to deal with emotion, not outsource it
- Rite of passage
- Coping with anxiety

Why were there any redundancies?

The redundancies that occurred in case study B were wholly legitimate. (This is in marked contrast to the 30%–50% redundancies planned in case study A, which was a figure plucked out of thin air to make the consultants feel good.) However, the business case for redundancies had nothing to do with the process that then occurred, the emotional and mental dynamic that surrounded the giving of the news to affected people as well as the management of the informal organization from then on (as opposed to the formal organization). The reasons for the redundancies were listed for me as:

- They were implicit and explicit in the operating model
- For savings
- It was a legitimate structure acceptable for business
- It was a more modern structure
- Always going to be an issue

Understanding redundancies: formal and psychological contract

One of the most useful and enduring concepts in the field of organizational behaviour is the 'psychological contract'. This is contrasted with the 'formal' or 'legal' contract. In the context of redundancy, both contracts are relevant.

Denise Rousseau (1990) describes two forms of contract, although she uses the terms 'transactional' (formal or legal) and 'relational' (psychological) (pp. 389–400).

> Psychological contracts are individual beliefs in reciprocal obligations between employees and employers. . . . Two types of obligation were demonstrated empirically: transactional obligations of high pay and career advancement in exchange for hard work; and relational obligations . . . job security for loyalty and a minimum length of stay. These types of obligations are connected with two forms of legal contracts: transactional and relational.
>
> (pp. 389–400)

In other words, her own research uncovered the obligations between employees and managers. These specific obligations might not be the same in other organizations. Note that the psychological obligations or contract is likely to be implicit.

In my experience and in the example of case study B I use in this chapter, the change team and managers **relied exclusively on the legal or formal contract**. They tended to completely ignore the psychological contract. The psychological contract embodies the set of expectations of the employer and those of the employee about how **they should behave to each other**. It is mostly implicit. It focuses on the relationship between the two and not on the contract between the two.

In the case I use in this chapter, the people I interviewed in that organization saw the psychological contracts as being out of operation. This has, however, important implications for the way employees felt about the redundancies.

The derivation of deep trauma

Theoretically, the psychological contract can be dealt with in a positive way or a negative way, as Figure 8.1 demonstrates. On the left, no attention is paid to the psychological contract and on the right is a positive psychological contract. If no psychological contract is in operation during the redundancy process, there could well be deep trauma. However, if the psychological contract, or relationship, is well managed, it is possible to see the redundancy in a positive light.

Two case studies of redundancy

Some people are immune to the effects of change. Most are not. I thought I was until I was personally affected.

In case study B, I was on the verge of redundancy twice and was once made redundant. Each time it was caused by an organizational push to shrink the HR branch to save money. The first time I was listed as an 'affected' person, my role was to go. I was sitting at my desk when the branch manager came up to me. People (i.e., fellow affected persons) had been called to one-on-one meetings all day to be told of their 'status'.

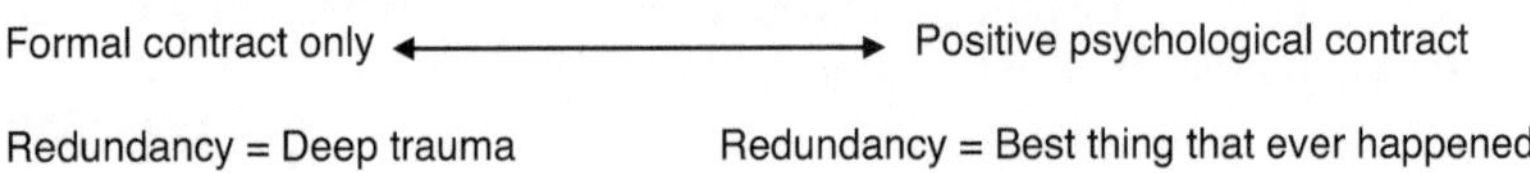

Figure 8.1 Psychological contracts around redundancy

I did not know at this stage that I was an affected person. It was my turn. She came right up to the front of my desk, looked me straight in the eye, leaned forward and gently said to me, "Do you think we could go outside for coffee?" Nobody else had had this privilege. I looked up at her and smiled, knowing what was up but appreciating the skilled way she had said it, and said, "Yes, I would like that". We started to walk to an outside café accompanied by another manager. We nattered about nothing very much, very personal. She was warm. After we had all sat down the second manager took over and said something like "you are an affected person". Just like that. I said, "Yes I know". He went on talking about the phasing of the process and she leaned across and said, "You realise you are an affected person". I said, "Yes, I realise that". My reaction had been so calm she must have thought I hadn't heard him. I was calm because she had made me calm with her behaviour. I had no upset whatsoever. She had dealt with me from a psychological contract; she had dealt with me as a human being not as an object. Not as an 'employee'. She was competent and decent, empathic. I had been taken to coffee because of my seniority. That was so reassuring. They didn't have to do it that way but they did. As a result, I had no negative views or feelings about the impending redundancy. The second manager there had been operating only from a formal contract; reading out the formal technicalities of times for consultation and so on.

As it was, I ended up with a newly created role anyway so I was not, in fact, made redundant, even though I was an 'affected' person for a while.

The second time I was, in fact, made redundant. This time it was different, gruesomely. We all knew there were to be redundancies this time; the HR branch had to save money. At about the time we were to know who was affected, one by one we were called in to a meeting in a small office room. This time I was asked to go to a meeting in a very correct but clipped, slightly cold manner. I became nervous going in. I was informed very quickly that I was an 'affected' person and that my role was up for being made redundant. This news was added to by a description of the specified phases of, for example, consultation etc. – my rights and obligations. The meeting was a classic version of a 'formal' contract and not a psychological contract. There was no warmth, no empathy, nothing human except when he explained that he had become an affected person himself. I left shattered and remained shattered for a year.

My explanation for the two reactions is that the former was highly skilled and human: it was a psychological contract in positive operation and the latter was unskilled and inhuman; it was without a psychological contract in operation.

Dealing with emotional things

There was an enormity of process factors that existed in case study B contrasted with the available skill in being able to cope with them. The consultants/change team were merely following procedures for what they were supposed to say. The consulting company knows (it must know?) it can't deal with emotional things. They use the word 'stress' instead – overuse it so you know they are uncomfortable with emotion. Person C in what follows is referring to the incompetence and cruelty of one of the senior managers involved in the change process.

> There was no justice for hearts. Be aware of the big gun machinery which doesn't care about you. Because so much [that happened] was on (a) being more efficient (b) cost-cutting. The way they delivered it did not seem very humane. For example, because of the way they communicated across the whole HR group. For example in one of the first meetings I became aware of the changes and their depth. But the manner in which it was delivered by the [manager] was [poor]. She presented very little information. She didn't have enough guts inside to explain to people who were affected. It was insensitive. They needed to be careful – we have mortgages and children, have to pay bills so she needed sensitivity. She said nothing . . . inhumane . . . The reaction to the change was to be surprised. I turned up one morning, knew nothing and my boss said "Can I have a talk with you?" It affects my life . . . but the way in which it was handled could have been better. . . . It's a vicious cycle. People have to really go at it and fight for themselves. I just want to be treated fairly. The process is wrong . . . The consultation process was a waste of time. It was a set-up. Just terrible. The change has been mismanaged. I don't feel there has been consideration or taking into account feelings. Inhuman. Inconsiderate of the feeling heart. Disbelief in how people were treated. Nasty and selfish.
>
> There was no real leadership and ownership of the change. I don't care how hard it is for [the manager]; it is her job to front up. She should have shown more empathy, and been proactive in assisting people . . . We are still made of ancient values.
>
> Person C

Outsourcing the emotional bits

There are several signs that the organization is unable to deal with the emotional aspects of the redundancies. The first was being confronted by pat, trite clichés. I became heartily sick of one senior manager who repeatedly told everyone he could how marvellous it had been to be redundant three times. I couldn't be bothered listening. Pascale stated,

> When disaster strikes, we are apt to be told . . . unhelpful clichés such as: "Hey, it's only a job," or "it happens to everyone," or "work should not have become so important to your life". Such self-talk is better at repressing feelings than at permitting a grieving process that creates emotional space for subsequent healing. Societal awareness must shift . . . so that the struggle to deal with disruptions in work is legitimised. Such a shift might serve to facilitate our quest for inner reciprocity, the ultimate source of spiritual and emotional development.
>
> (Pascale et al., 2000, p. 267)

Emotional skills and IQ skills – treat me as if I have a brain and a heart

In case B, we were confronted not only with a void in terms of a psychological contract but also a complete absence of EQ (emotional quotient) and IQ (intellectual quotient). Because they were unable to deal with the psychological or emotional angle, they repeatedly finished their talk sessions with the news that we could go to an outplacement company – anyone who was 'stressed'.

The outplacement company was even more inept than the consulting company case study B had hired. I went for three sessions. In each of them, we went through the same routine. I would tell the counsellor that I wanted to do something radical once I had left the organization. She, in turn, would indicate to me that she disapproved of anything so radical and counsel me to try to re-hire myself into the government which, to me, was into a bureaucracy that I was still unfamiliar with and uncomfortable with after spending four years there. Also, I had never liked being an employee and didn't want to prolong the experience, but she was unable to take this feeling seriously. In sum, it was all a complete waste of time.

No redundancy is simple. The question is how it is done. You can't rely on outsourcing the soft bit. In any event, the damage might already have been done. You can't outsource the way the manager speaks to you or the GM of the branch speaks to you or does or does not do the weekly stand up. The change team and the senior managers were never held to account for their incompetence or cruelty. The agenda was simply to get through the formal and legal requirements and that was their change programme.

Rite of passage: the breadth of redundancy

This matters because redundancy has a bigger meaning. It is not just another event in the life or career cycle of an individual. It is a rite of passage. This rite of passage occurs when an individual leaves one group (role) and social situation to another (role) and social situation. However, redundancy is not simply about going from one job to another with, hopefully, a short transition in between. The rite of passage affects all levels, as can be seen in Figure 8.2. It impacts spiritual, emotional, mental and physical spheres in our lives. It is not a simple phenomenon.

> No one spoke to us. Got a letter from my boss. The manager responsible didn't front up to those made redundant. Cowardly approach for affected staff. No exit process entered into by the boss. No celebration of life in service. No attempt to help people affected by the transition out of the organization or to give due recognition for contributions . . . Total disrespect and failure to recognise that people have relationships to maintain . . . I became invisible. Unconscionable. Demeaning.
>
> Person D

This person's focus is not just his role, but his whole life. He wants his long years of life in service recognized, but they were not.

To resolve the redundancy situation for those affected, managers need also to address all four spheres. That they are real means some people manage to make enormous lateral moves after redundancy: it has affected them in all four spheres.

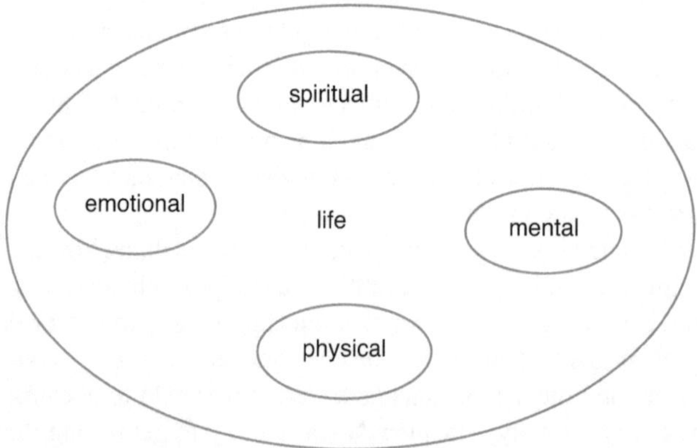

Figure 8.2 Rite of passage

Coping

If handled correctly, the functional responses to anxiety, even to an event like redundancy, can move you along a change process.

Some of the most interesting work done on anxiety is by Karen Horney (1945). She describes three different kinds of responses to anxiety: Moving Away, Moving Against and Moving Towards. The healthy strategy (Wiki) is called Moving With. The defensive strategies are the first three and are to protect themselves. The latter is when psychologically healthy people develop relationships through such things as communication, compromise etc.

All responses can be positive if they stem from basic underlying assumptions of wellness rather than illness (adapted from Garden, 2015). Table 8.1 illustrates.

In case study B, the three anxiety-based reactions were apparent in the redundant employees, but also in the change team. The lead person from the consulting company was a Moving Against person; up against a question, he would frequently respond with aggression or be argumentative. This less-than-functional response affected the change process considerably. Similarly, the HR branch manager, who was temporary, had an anxiety response of Moving Away and was noted for cancelling the weekly stand up meeting in the middle of the change process. The change leader himself was a Moving Towards person, reaching out to make contact with many people, but in an inappropriate way. For the employees on the receiving end of these behaviours, there was likewise a mix of the four responses to anxiety.

All of us struggled to get to the Moving With response; some more successfully than others. The acid test was and is forging of successful healthy relationships. This, however, was as true of the redundancy response as it was of any change efforts, the province of this book, in general. Without them, we have the eight deadly sins preventing effective change, and with them, we have the opposite blessings of organization change.

Table 8.1 Coping with anxiety

	Moving against	*Moving Towards*	*Moving Away*	*Moving With*
Illness assumptions	Aggression, belittling, manic	Overly social, burdensome	Retreats, runs away	No illness assumptions
Wellness assumptions	Proactive, enduring	Sociable, people gatherer	Creating space, independent	Creating healthy relationships

Ten questions on the deep trauma of redundancy

1 When have you experienced a redundancy gone well? What was it like?

....

....

2 When have you experienced a redundancy gone poorly? What was it like?

....

....

3 How do you think people typically react?

....

....

4 What triggers that reaction (good or bad)?

....

....

5 How is it helpful to think of a formal/legal contract and a psychological contract?

....

....

6 Can you imagine progressing straight to a healthy positive state?

....

....

7 Have you been through a rite of passage?

....

....

8 If so, how did you negotiate it so it worked out well?

....

....

9 Do you treat redundant people with respect or as if they have done something wrong?

....

....

10 How do you cope with anxiety: Moving Away, Moving Towards, Moving Against or Moving With?

....

....

Checklist 8.1 On yourself

This is a checklist of 10 questions for others to answer about **yourself** to the handling of redundancies. Feel free to copy the checklist and use. Distribute to a minimum of 10 people. The context is any redundancies you or your organization have been or are engaged in.

	1 *Minimal*	*2*	*3*	*4* *Average*	*5*	*6*	*7* *Brilliant*
1 Do I make use of the psychological contract, not just the legal/formal contract?							
2 Do I understand how important redundancy is?							
3 Do I understand that people can be in deep trauma?							
4 Do I know how to support people through the experience?							
5 Do I front up enough to people who have been made redundant							
6 Do I avoid self-help truisms when dealing with redundancies?							
7 Do I treat redundant people with respect?							
8 Do I try to deal with the emotional reactions myself, not solely outsource to outside suppliers?							
9 Do I handle the whole process as a rite of passage?							
10 Do I cope with anxiety well?							

Checklist 8.2 On the change team

This is a checklist of 10 questions for others to answer about the **change team** to gauge the handling of redundancies. Feel free to copy the checklist and use. Distribute to a minimum of 10 people. The context is any redundancies they or your organization have been or are engaged in.

	1	*2*	*3*	*4*	*5*	*6*	*7*
	Minimal			*Average*			*Brilliant*
1 Does the change team make use of the psychological contract, not just the formal/legal contract?							
2 Does the change team understand how important redundancy is?							
3 Does the change team understand that people can be in deep trauma?							
4 Does the change team know how to support people through the experience?							
5 Does the change team front up enough to people who have been made redundant?							
6 Does the change team avoid glib self-help truisms when dealing with redundancy?							
7 Does the change team treat redundant people with respect?							
8 Does the change team try to deal with emotional reactions themselves, not solely outsource to outside organizations?							
9 Does the change team handle the whole process as a rite of passage?							
10 Do you cope well with anxiety?							

Checklist 8.3 On the senior management team

This is a checklist of 10 questions for others to answer about the **senior management team** to gauge handling of redundancies. Feel free to copy the checklist and use. Distribute to a minimum of 20 people. The context is any redundancies they or your organization have been or are engaged in.

	1	*2*	*3*	*4*	*5*	*6*	*7*
	Minimal			*Average*			*Brilliant*
1 Does the senior management team make use of the psychological contract, not just the formal/legal contract?							
2 Does the senior management team understand how important redundancy is?							
3 Does the senior management team understand that people can be in deep trauma?							
4 Does the senior management team know how to support people through the experience?							
5 Does the senior management team front up enough to people who have been made redundant?							
6 Does the senior management team avoid glib self-help truisms when dealing with redundancy?							
7 Does the senior management team treat redundant people with respect?							
8 Does the senior management team try to deal with emotional reactions themselves, not solely outsource to outside organizations?							

(*Continued*)

(Continued)

	1	*2*	*3*	*4*	*5*	*6*	*7*
	Minimal			*Average*			*Brilliant*
9 Does the senior management team handle the whole process as a rite of passage?							
10 Does the senior management team cope well with anxiety?							

References

Amis, J., Slack, T. and Hinings, C. R. (2004). The pace, sequence and linearity of radical change. *Academy of Management Journal*. 47, 1, 15–39.

Beer, M. and Nohria, N. (2011). Cracking the code of change. In *Change management: HBR's 10 must reads*. Harvard Business Review Press, Boston, MA.

Berne, E. (1964). *Games people play*. Ballantine Books, New York.

Burke, W. W. (2014). *Organization change: Theory and practice*. 4th edition. Sage, Thousand Oaks, CA.

Capra, F. (1996). *The web of life*. Anchor Books, New York.

Capra, F. and Luigi, P. (2014). *The systems view of life*. Cambridge University Press, Cambridge, UK.

Dent, E. B. and Goldberg, S. G. (1999). Challenging resistance to change. *Journal of Applied Behavioural Science*. 35, 1, 25–41.

Di Fonzo, N. and Brasho, P. (1998). A tale of two corporations: Managing uncertainty during organization change. *HR Management*. Fall/Winter, 37, 3 + 4, 295–303.

Ford, J. D., Ford, L. W. and d'Ameilio, A. (2008). Resistance to change: The rest of the story. *Academy of Management Review*. 33, 2, 362–377.

Garden, A. (2000). *Reading the mind of the organization*. Gower Publishing Limited, Hampshire, England.

Garden, A. (2015). *Roles of organization development*. Gower Publishing Limited, Hampshire, England.

Garvin, D. A. and Roberto, M. A. (2011). Change through persuasion. In *On change management: HBR's 10 must reads*. Harvard Business Review Press, Boston, MA.

Gersick, C. J. G. (1991). Revolutionary change theories: A multilevel exploration of the punctuated equilibrium paradigm. The Academy of Management Review. 16, 1, 10–36.

Hamel, G. and Zanini, M. (2014). *Build a change platform not a change programme*. Mckinsey and Co. Insights and publications.

Horney, K. (1945). *Our inner conflicts*. W.W. Norton and Company, New York, NY.

Jung, C. G. (1971). *Psychological types*. Collected works vol. 16. Bollinger series. Princeton University Press, Princeton, NJ.

Kauffman, S. (1995). *At home in the universe*. Oxford University Press, Oxford, England.

Kotter, J. P. and Cohen, D. S. (1995). *The heart of change*. Harvard Business Review Press, Boston, MA.

Kotter, J. P. and Cohen, D. S. (2002). *Leading change: On change management*. Harvard Business Review Press, Boston, MA.

Langer, E. J. (1989). *Mindfulness*. Perseus Books Group, Cambridge, MA.

Lewin, K. (1947). Group decision and social change. In E. E. Macoby and E. L. Hartley (Eds.). *Readings in social psychology*. Henry Holt, New York.

Lines, R. (2005). How social accounting and participation during change affect organizational learning. *Journal of Workplace Learning*. 17, 3, 157–177.

Mele, A. (2001). *Self-deception unmasked*. Princeton University Press, Princeton, NJ.

Micklethwait, J. and Wooldridge, A. (1996). *The witch doctors*. Times Business, New York, NY.

Myers, I., McCaulley, M. H., Quenk, N. and Hammer, A. L. (2009). *MBTI manual*. 3rd edition. Consulting Psychologists Press, Mountain View, CA.

Pascale, R. T., Milleman, M. and Gioja, C. (2000). *Surfing the edge of chaos*. Three Rivers Press, New York, NY.

PwC April (2012). 1. p. 1.

Rousseau, D. (1990). New hire perceptions of their own and their employer's obligations: A study of psychological contracts. *Journal of Organizational Behavior*, 11, 389–400.

Schutz, W. (1984). *The truth option*. Ten Speed Press, Berkeley, CA.

Syantek, D. J. (1997). Order out of chaos: Nonlinear systems and organization change. *Current topics in management*. vol. 2, 167–188.

Wanberg, C. R. and Banas, J. T. (2000). Predictors and outcomes of open ness to changes in a reorganizing workplace. *Journal of Applied Psychology*. 85, 132–142.

Weick, K. E. and Quinn, R. E. (1999). Organization change and development. *Annual Review of Psychology*. 50, 361–386.

Wittig, C. (2005). Employees reactions to organizational change. *Organization Development Practitioner*. 44, 2.

Index

For Product Safety Concerns and Information please contact our EU representative GPSR@taylorandfrancis.com Taylor & Francis Verlag GmbH, Kaufingerstraße 24, 80331 München, Germany